GRILLO'S PICKLES
I ♥ GRILLO'S PICKLES

I ♥ GRILLO'S PICKLES
GRILLO'S PICKLES

GRILLO'S

PRESENTS

PICKLED

GRILLO'S

PRESENTS

PICKLED

100 PICKLE-CENTRIC RECIPES *TO* CHANGE YOUR LIFE

ABRAMS, NEW YORK

GRILLO'S
PICKLES

CONTENTS

Chapter 4

ALL THINGS FRIED

Chapter 5

SANDWICH LOVERS

Chapter 6

DON'T GRILL WITHOUT GRILLO'S

Chapter 7

THE MAIN ATTRACTION

50
40
30
20
10
GRILLO'S PICKLES
FRESH
HOT
Italian Dill Spears
GRILLO'S PICKLES
FRESH

FOREWORD

This cookbook is dedicated to the people who have gotten us where we are—the Grillo's fans. The true believers, the pickle lovers, the people who got Sam Sam tattoos, and the people who didn't blink when their friends said that they were getting Sam Sam tattoos. Every jar you bought, every time you shared Grillo's with someone, every nice message or post, a pickle grew its wings. Without you, we'd still be hawking pickles at the Park Street T stop. So, thank you.

We love you. We're not getting a tattoo of your face anytime soon, but we love you.

INTRODUCTION

PICKLES.

Love 'em or hate 'em, they've stood the test of time and have been around for more than four thousand years. It all started long ago when the ancient Mesopotamians decided to store their cucumbers in an acidic brine for preservation. Pickles and pickling have since been introduced to cultures all around the world sparking delicious flavors and techniques for picklers to pass down to future generations and experiment with on their own.

Today, pickles have reached near celebrity status. Whether it's crazed pickle fans flocking to the next pickle-flavored snack, or your favorite athlete drinking pickle juice on the sidelines, they're everywhere.

Our story is a little different. Grillo's Pickles began in 2008 out of a hand-built wooden pickle cart and a hundred-year-old family recipe. Every morning, we sold two spears for a dollar out of the cart. Every morning, the cart would get wheeled down to the Park Street T stop in the Boston Common where we'd spend the better part of the day hustling pickles, wrapped in tin foil. This was back in the day when street vendors in Boston were serving up fried dough, sausages, ice cream, and lemonade. Grillo's brought something fresh and exciting to the street, even if some people doubted that we'd make it as a business. In fact, the city of Boston thought the pickle cart was such a wild idea they laughed and gave us the vendor license for free. (Thanks for the vote of confidence.) Rain or shine, we were out there selling pickles to as many people as we could, every day. Friends would come by the cart and hang around and tell stories or play cards, and it always felt like a home away from home to us.

After the *Boston Globe* wrote an article about Grillo's and called our pickles "the best they've ever had," we got approached by Whole Foods Market to see if we would consider selling in their Cambridge, Massachusetts, location. We didn't have UPCs or nutrition facts, we didn't have corrugated cases, and we didn't have a way to get product to stores. Most worrisome, we were still making and hand-packing our pickles one jar at a time at night when we weren't selling in the park. But, what we lacked in process we made up for in hustle. We had four employees and a van. We packed our pickles in wonton soup containers we bought from a Chinese restaurant supply wholesaler (they fit our cucumbers and came pre-sterilized). We repurposed discarded pineapple crates from the produce market and hand-delivered the pickles to the shelves ourselves. Luckily, once they got to the shelves, people bought them. And the rest, as they say, is history.

In addition to pickles, Grillo's has done everything from pickle-flavored ice cream, to beer, potato chips, and hummus. Plus, we've done some epic collabs including a pair of Patrick Ewing sneakers, a sterling silver chain with Good Art, and even a custom Polaroid camera.

It's clear that people are obsessed with pickles and we'd like to think Grillo's had a little bit to do with that. Don't get it twisted, we know that pickles have some haters, too. We all have that one friend who won't eat the pickle and another who will gladly take it off their plate, but this book isn't for them.

This book is for the pickle lovers. The pickle people who are always looking for that next innovative recipe using their favorite Grillo's flavor. At its heart, Grillo's has always been about having fun with your chosen family. We're proud to continue creating quality products that you feel good about feeding to those you hold close.

To everyone who's been with us on this pickle-fueled trip, whether you've been with us since day one or just discovered us at your local grocery store: We thank you, and we're happy to have you enjoy our pickles. Grillo's has always been about having fun and creating quality products that you're proud to feed to your friends and family.

GRILLO'S
PICKLES

GRILLO'S × CHEF RAPH

We first met Chef Raph back in 2021 when he helped us out during our party for National Pickle Day at Ray's Bar in the Lower East Side of New York City. We featured limited pickle cocktails with our Grillo's dill pickles as well as some menu items like fried pickles, Cuban sliders, and Reuben egg rolls.

The food was such a hit that Chef Raph started to run out of components and started free-styling on the spot some insane recipes with our pickles. Watching him was like watching an artist throwing paint on a canvas, creating something unlike anything we'd ever seen.

This book is meant to encapsulate that night at Ray's Bar with pickle-inspired recipes straight from Chef Raph's brain and onto your plates. We hope you love eating them as much as we loved creating them!

Chill out. Eat a Pickle.
Grillo's Pickles

SAM SAM WAS FIRST BORN FROM A WOODEN PICKLE CART NESTLED IN THE BUSY STREETS OF DOWNTOWN BOSTON.

From his inception, Sam Sam was always cooler than a cucumber—he was one cold, chillin' pickle. Much more than just our beloved mascot, Sam Sam truly represents the very essence of the Grillo's Pickles brand. His demeanor is perpetually laid-back with an aura that resonates positive vibes, and he's become the ultimate emblem of optimism, joy, and PICKLES.

Always up for a good time, Sam Sam's infectious spirit breathes life into every party he graces. His journeys around the country have made him a beloved figure, with tales of his escapades whispered from state to state. No matter how popular he becomes, Sam Sam never forgets where he came from and remains a true pickle for the people. Sam Sam's rise from a simple pickle cart to national icon speaks volumes of his charisma and the bond he shares with pickle people everywhere.

GRILLO'S

2 SPEARS $1
GRILLO'S
PICKLES
GRILLO'S PICKLES
HOT

FRESH

SAM SAM'S

FUN FACT

AMERICANS CONSUME ABOUT 9 POUNDS (4 KG) OF PICKLES PER PERSON EVERY YEAR. THIS COOKBOOK SHOULD HELP GET THAT NUMBER TO A REASONABLE 20 POUNDS (9 KG) OF PICKLES PER PERSON EVERY YEAR.

CRISP
CLEAN
FRESH

Chapter 1

AT HOME PICKLING

There are lots of ways to pickle. Do you prefer sweet bread and butter, apple cider vinegar, or a quick-pickle? Maybe you prefer carrots to cucumbers, or want to experiment with your own backyard veggies. No matter your pickle preference, pickling can be a fun family activity for one or many—and might even be something you'll pass on through generations, like our very own Grillo's Pickle recipe.

These are our favorite classic and out of-the-box pickling recipes.

P. Cauliflower 4/30

P. Green TOMATO 4/30
P. Cucumbers 4/30
P. CARROTTS 4/30

BASIC BRINE

Makes 3 cups (720 ml)

The great thing about brines is how personalized you can make them! Rice wine vinegar is Chef Raph's favorite to use for a basic brine, while champagne vinegar adds a nice sweetness. You can also use lots of different vegetables, like cauliflower, radishes, and jalapeños!

In a saucepan, combine 1 cup (240 ml) water, the vinegar, sugar, salt, dill, bay leaves, and garlic and bring to a boil. Stuff a Mason jar or an airtight container with your vegetables of choice, then pour the hot brine into the jar. Let cool, then cover with the lid and store in the refrigerator for up to 3 months.

Ingredients

2 cups (480 ml) vinegar (your favorite)

½ cup (100 g) sugar

2 teaspoons salt

1 sprig fresh dill

2 bay leaves

5 garlic cloves

Vegetables

GRILLO'S CHICKEN BRINE

Makes 3 cups (720 ml)

Why let leftover pickle brine go to waste when you can use it to keep your chicken moist and flavorful? We dare you to replace the turkey this holiday season.

In a saucepan, stir together 4 cups (960 ml) water, the pickle brine, lemon slices, pickle chips, fennel seeds, and bay leaves. Bring to a boil and let simmer over low heat for 20 minutes or until fragrant. Let cool and store in an airtight container in the refrigerator for up to 1 week.

Ingredients

2 cups (480 ml) Grillo's pickle brine

1 lemon, cut into thin slices

5 Grillo's pickle chips

1 tablespoon fennel seeds

2 bay leaves

Pickled Watermelon Rinds
Jerk Pickled Pineapple

PICKLED WATERMELON RINDS

Makes 2 cups (480 ml)

- 2 cups (360 g) watermelon rinds, cut into bite-size rectangles
- 2 cups (480 ml) Basic Brine (page 20)

Place the watermelon rinds in a Mason jar or an airtight container. In a saucepan, bring the brine to a boil and pour over the watermelon rinds. Let cool, then cover with the lid and store in the refrigerator for up to 3 months.

JERK PICKLED PINEAPPLE

Makes 4 cups (480 ml) pineapple and brine

- 2 cups (330 g) finely diced fresh pineapple
- 2 cups (480 ml) Make It Hot Brine (page 27)
- 3 tablespoons Homemade Jerk Spice (recipe follows) or store-bought

Preheat a skillet until very hot. Add the pineapple and char on one side until a deep brown, about 5 minutes.

Meanwhile, in a small saucepan, bring the pickle brine and jerk spice to a boil.

Pour over the charred pineapple. Let cool and store in an airtight container in the refrigerator for up to 3 months.

HOMEMADE JERK SPICE

Makes about ⅔ cup (190 g)

- 1 tablespoon onion powder
- 1 tablespoon garlic powder
- 2 teaspoons cayenne pepper
- 2 teaspoons salt
- 2 teaspoons freshly ground black pepper
- 2 teaspoons dried thyme
- 2 teaspoons brown sugar
- 1 teaspoon ground allspice
- 1 teaspoon paprika
- 1 teaspoon red pepper flakes
- ½ teaspoon ground cloves
- ½ teaspoon ground nutmeg
- ¼ teaspoon ground cumin

Place all the seasonings and spices in a medium bowl and mix until fully combined. Store in an airtight container for up to a year.

PICKLED GREEN TOMATOES

Makes 2 cups (480 ml)

- 2 cups (360 g) small-dice green tomatoes
- 2 cups (480 ml) Basic Brine (page 20)
- 3 cardamom pods
- 2 whole star anise

Place the green tomatoes in a Mason jar or an airtight container. In a saucepan, combine the brine, cardamom, and star anise and bring to a boil. Pour over the tomatoes. Let cool, then cover with the lid and store in the refrigerator for up to 3 months.

PICKLED MUSTARD SEEDS

Makes about ⅓ cup (75 ml)

- ⅓ cup (57 g) mustard seeds
- 1 cup (240 ml) Basic Brine (page 20)
- 1 tablespoon brown sugar

In a small saucepan, combine the mustard seeds and 1 cup (240 ml) water and bring to a boil. Drain in a fine-mesh sieve and repeat this step one more time to reduce bitterness.

In the same saucepan, combine the blanched mustard seeds, brine, and brown sugar. Bring to a low simmer and cook until the majority of the brine has been absorbed, about 15 minutes. Remove from the heat and let cool before storing in an airtight container in the refrigerator.

MAKE IT HOT BRINE

Makes 3 cups (720 ml)

Try using apple cider vinegar if you want to experiment with something new. You can also change the ratio to add one more cup (240 ml) of vinegar if you want your veggies more acidic. We love to throw in pearl onions, banana peppers, and crunchy cabbage!

In a saucepan, combine 1 cup (240 ml) water, the vinegar, sugar, salt, dill, bay leaves, garlic, cayenne, and chiles and bring to a boil. Stuff a Mason jar or an airtight container with your vegetables of choice, then pour the hot brine over the vegetables. Let cool, then cover with the lid and store in the refrigerator for up to 3 months.

Ingredients

2 cups (480 ml) vinegar (your favorite)

½ cup (100 g) sugar

2 teaspoons salt

1 sprig fresh dill

2 bay leaves

5 garlic cloves

1 teaspoon cayenne pepper

2 medium Fresno chile peppers, halved

Vegetables

CRISP

SUPER FRESH UPER CRISPY

SAM SAM'S

FUN FACT

DID YOU KNOW THAT PICKLES KEEP YOU BEAUTIFUL? IT IS SAID THAT CLEOPATRA WAS A BIG PICKLE GIRL AND THAT SHE WOULD EAT THEM TO HELP KEEP HER GORGEOUS. I GUESS TIKTOK IS RIGHT . . . HOT GIRLS REALLY DO EAT PICKLES.

FFFRESHHH

Chapter 2

SNACK HACKS

We've made it our mission to change the pickle game and the way people think about pickles. No longer is the pickle an afterthought, relegated to the side of the plate or the supporting role of occasional hamburger topper—it's your new best friend. Plus, pickles are a great way to satisfy your snack craving, no matter what time of day it is.

While a fresh Grillo's pickle is the perfect snack on its own, we encourage you to step outside the jar and try some of these snack hacks for yourself.

We promise they'll have you coming back again and again for just "one more bite."

CRISPY PICKLE CHEESE CRACKERS

Serves 6

A mouthful, but in all the best ways. These pickle-y, cheesy crackers are ready in minutes and will shut down the entire party for being too tasty.

Preheat the oven to 350°F (180°C). Line two baking sheets with parchment paper and coat with cooking spray.

Lay 24 piles of shredded cheese (about 2 tablespoons each), leaving 2 inches (5 cm) border between them. Place one pickle chip in the center of each pile.

Bake until the cheese is golden brown and crispy, 10 to 12 minutes. Let cool and enjoy.

Ingredients

2 cups (230 g) shredded Cheddar cheese

24 Grillo's pickle chips

GRILLO'S
PICKLES

H+C+P SNACK WRAP

Serves 4

The ideal after-school or after-work snack that won't ruin your dinner, this upgrade to the traditional ham and cheese sammy will please even the pickiest of eaters. Plus, it mostly uses ingredients that you probably already have on hand.

For each roll, lay 2 slices of ham on top of one another. Spread with a generous amount of yellow mustard and top with 1 slice of cheese. Place 1 Grillo's pickle spear in the center and roll up tightly. Continue with another layer of mustard and cheese.

Place the bread slices on a flat surface and use a rolling pin to flatten. Roll the ham and cheese in the bread tightly and skewer on both ends to secure. Repeat the process.

In a medium skillet, heat the butter over medium heat. Add the roll-ups and brown all sides evenly, about 6 minutes. Serve hot and enjoy!

Ingredients

- 16 slices deli ham
- 4 tablespoons (60 ml) yellow mustard
- 16 slices Swiss cheese
- 8 Grillo's pickle spears
- 4 slices white sandwich bread
- 18 small wooden skewers
- 2 tablespoons butter

BRINY TATER SALAD

Serves 4 to 6

The best things in life begin with P. You've got potatoes, pickles, puppies, and plenty more. Why not combine a couple and see where it takes you? Using leftover pickle brine has never been easier than when you add it to a solid potato salad recipe. This recipe uses crunchy minced shallots and chives for added flavor, and salty pickle brine to make it shine.

In a large soup pot, combine 4 cups (960 ml) water, the pickle brine, and potatoes. Bring the liquid to a boil and cook potatoes until tender, 10 minutes. Drain and when cool enough to handle, quarter the potatoes.

Transfer to a bowl and add the rémoulade, shallots, chives, salt and pepper to taste, and olive oil. Refrigerate until serving time and serve chilled, garnished with chile powder and oregano leaves.

Ingredients

4 cups (960 ml) Grillo's pickle brine or Basic Brine (page 20)

3 pounds (1.4 kg) baby potatoes

¼ cup (60 ml) Rémoulade (page 64)

2 tablespoons minced shallots

¼ cup (11 g) minced fresh chives

Salt and freshly ground black pepper

2 tablespoons olive oil

Chile powder

Fresh oregano leaves

Green with Envy Sandwiches
(page 38)
Pickle Nacho Cheese
(page 207)
Bacon-Wrapped
Pickles (page 39)

Jerk Pickled Pineapple
(page 25)
Please, Please, Can I
Have a Pickle Grilled
Cheese? (page 49)

GREEN *with* ENVY SANDWICHES

Serves 4

No bread? No problem. These fun pickle sandwiches are better without it. These delicious ham sandwiches are made with dill pickle chips instead of bread.

Layer 1 pickle chip, 2 slices deli ham, 1 slice Swiss cheese, ½ tablespoon yellow mustard, another pickle chip, and then skewer. Repeat and enjoy.

Ingredients

- 8 Grillo's pickle chips
- 8 slices deli ham
- 4 slices Swiss cheese
- 2 tablespoons yellow mustard
- 4 small skewers

BACON-WRAPPED PICKLES

Serves 4

Bacon AND pickles? How can you go wrong? This is a savory, crunch-packed snack unlike any other. Pigs in a blanket, step aside, there's a new sheriff in town.

Pour 6 inches (15 cm) oil into a dutch oven and heat to 350°F (177°C).

Meanwhile, wrap each pickle spear in 1½ slices of bacon and place two skewers on both sides of the pickle on a perpendicular angle (they should look like goal posts).

Add the pickles to the hot oil and cook until the bacon is cooked through and crispy, about 4 minutes.

Ingredients

- Vegetable oil, for deep-frying
- 4 Grillo's pickle spears
- 6 slices bacon
- 8 medium wooden skewers

SMOKED TROUT DIP

Serves 4

Smoked trout? No doubt! A firm yet flaky fish with a mild sweetness to it that is undeniably delicious. Don't get it twisted, the pickles are still up for an Oscar, but we'll let the trout be the star of this dish (this time . . .).

Ingredients

- ¼ cup (30 g) minced shallots
- ½ cup (140 g) chopped Grillo's pickles
- 1 tablespoon Grillo's pickle brine
- 11 ounces (310 g) smoked trout, shredded (about 2 cups)
- ⅓ cup (75 ml) sour cream
- 2 ounces (55 g) cream cheese
- 4 tablespoons (11 g) minced fresh chives
- Salt and freshly ground black pepper
- 1 teaspoon paprika, for garnish
- Toasted bread or crackers, for serving

In a small bowl, combine the shallots, pickles, and brine and marinate for 20 minutes.

In a medium bowl, combine the smoked trout, sour cream, cream cheese, marinated shallot-pickle mixture (don't strain), 2 tablespoons of the chives, and salt and pepper to taste. Garnish with the remaining 2 tablespoons chives and the paprika. Finish with more black pepper. Serve with your favorite toasted bread or crackers.

NOT YOUR AVERAGE PICKLE GUACAMOLE

Serves 4

We'd pay extra for this guac. Up your guac game by adding some Grillo's hot Pickle de Gallo and watch your homies finish the whole batch.

In a bowl, combine the avocados, the Pickle de Gallo, lime juice, and cilantro and break the avocados with a spoon until creamy. Season with salt to taste. If desired, sprinkle with Tajín. Serve with tortilla chips.

Ingredients

3 avocados, diced

3 tablespoons Grillo's Hot Pickle de Gallo

2 tablespoons fresh lime juice

¼ cup (10 g) chopped fresh cilantro

Salt

1 teaspoon Tajín seasoning, for sprinkling (optional)

Tortilla chips, for serving

Not Your Average Pickle Guacamole (page 41)

PICKLE BOATS

Serves 8

Hop in! No life jacket needed. These pickle boats have a little bit of everything to make each bite the perfect bite.

Measure out 2 tablespoons each of the bacon and scallions and set aside for garnish.

In a bowl, combine the cream cheese, remaining bacon and scallions, and chopped pickles and mix until well incorporated.

Fill each pickle boat with the cheese filling and garnish with the reserved bacon and scallions and a sprinkling of paprika.

Ingredients

½ cup (120 g) crumbled cooked bacon (from about 8 slices raw)

½ cup (50 g) chopped scallions

4 ounces (115 g) cream cheese, at room temperature

½ cup (140 g) chopped Grillo's pickles

4 Grillo's whole kosher dill pickles, halved lengthwise and cored (to make boats)

Paprika, for sprinkling

PRIZED PICKLE HUMMUS

Serves 4

We live in a world that has pickle hummus and that's good enough for me. Transform boring old hummus into delicious briny pickle hummus with this staple recipe. It's so good that you'll be licking the plate.

In a food processor, combine the chickpeas, pickle brine, lime juice, lemon juice, tahini, garlic, ice cubes, olive oil, and cumin and blend until very smooth. Adjust the consistency with warm water and more olive oil if needed. Add salt and pepper to taste.

Transfer the hummus to a bowl. Fold in the chopped pickles and finish with crumbled pita chips. Serve with pita chips.

Ingredients

1 (15-ounce/425 g) can chickpeas, drained

2 tablespoons Grillo's pickle brine

¼ cup (60 ml) fresh lime juice

¼ cup (60 ml) fresh lemon juice

¼ cup (60 ml) well-stirred tahini

1 small garlic clove, minced

3 ice cubes

2 tablespoons extra-virgin olive oil, plus more as needed

1 teaspoon ground cumin

2 tablespoons warm water

Salt and freshly ground black pepper

½ cup (140 g) chopped Grillo's pickles

Crumbled pita chips, for garnish

Pita chips, for dipping

PLEASE, PLEASE, CAN I HAVE A PICKLE GRILLED CHEESE?

Serves 4

Just when you thought grilled cheese couldn't get any better. Who knew that adding pickles to a grilled cheese would be such a game changer? Well, we did actually.

In a bowl, stir together the butter and Cheddar. Season with salt and pepper and set aside.

Build each sandwich with a schmear of the butter-Cheddar mixture on the inside of both slices of bread, American cheese, and 3 Sandwich Makers. Close the sandwiches.

Preheat a nonstick pan over medium heat. Sear each sandwich until golden brown on both sides, about 3 minutes per side. Make sure to clean your pan between searing. Cut on a diagonal and enjoy.

Ingredients

1 stick (4 ounces/115 g) unsalted butter, at room temperature

2 cups (230 g) shredded Cheddar cheese

Salt and freshly ground black pepper

8 slices white bread

2 cups (230 g) shredded American cheese

12 Grillo's Sandwich Makers

GRILLO'S PICKLES
FRESH
Pickle Spears

GRILLO'S CRUDITÉS

Serves 4

Great for grazing, crudités will up your hosting game by 100. Veggie lovers will appreciate the extra effort of this platter, and the Green Goddess Dressing is sure to be a hit.

Arrange the vegetables and pickles on a plate and serve with a bowl of green goddess dressing.

Ingredients

5 ounces (140 g) carrot sticks (about 1 cup)

4 ounces (115 g) celery sticks (about 1 cup)

12 Grillo's pickle spears

½ cup (120 ml) Green Goddess Dressing (page 201)

SAM SAM'S

FUN FACT

THIS ONE IS FOR OUR PHILLY FAMILY! THE PHILADELPHIA EAGLES USED PICKLE JUICE TO BEAT THE COWBOYS. WITH TEMPS HITTING 109°F (43°C) ON SEPTEMBER 3, 2000, PHILADELPHIA PLAYERS CHUGGED PICKLE JUICE AND GAVE CREDIT TO THE ALMIGHTY PICKLE BRINE FOR THEIR 41–14 WIN.

Chapter 3

PPP (PERFECT PICKLE PLATES)

If a pickle is on a plate in our house, it's getting eaten. In this chapter, we're giving the pickle people what they deserve—a bunch of banging recipes that star the pickle. Perfect for hosting, munching, crunching, grazing, and nibbling, these shared plates are sure to be a hit with the whole squad.

BIG M*C FLATBREAD

Serves 4 to 6

It's a burger, it's a flatbread, it's a Grillo's Big M*c flatbread! Can't choose between pizza or burgers for dinner? Have both. This flatbread recipe is the perfect way to soothe your "big mac" craving in the comfort of your own home. The harmonious combination of beef, sauce, and pickles can't be beat!

PRO TIP: Cook it on a pizza stone to make it extra crispy.

Preheat the oven to 425°F (220°C).

Preheat a large cast-iron skillet over high heat.

In a bowl, season the ground beef with the Sazón and salt. Spread the seasoned beef on both flatbreads. Add the flatbreads beef side down to the skillet and sear until a deep brown crust develops, about 4 minutes.

Set the flatbreads on a sheet pan and top with the mozzarella and American cheese. Transfer to the oven and roast until crispy and golden brown, about 5 minutes.

Top with burger sauce, diced onion, shredded lettuce, pickles, and sesame seeds. Portion each with a pizza cutter into 6 even pieces.

Ingredients

- ½ pound (225 g) ground beef
- 2 tablespoons Sazón seasoning
- 1 tablespoon salt
- 2 Pickle Perfect Flatbreads (page 79)
- 1 cup (110 g) shredded low-moisture mozzarella cheese
- ½ cup (55 g) diced American cheese
- ¼ cup (60 ml) Grillo's Burger Sauce (page 206)
- ¼ cup (30 g) small-dice onion, soaked in cold water
- ½ cup (30 g) thinly shredded lettuce
- 1 (16-ounce/473 ml) container Grillo's pickle chips
- 1 tablespoon sesame seeds

Big M*c Flatbread (page 55)

IN A PICKLE WEDGE SALAD

Serves 4

Grillo's ranch dressing gives this wedge a leg up on other salads. When a run-of-the-mill wedge just won't cut it, our dressing adds an extra bite to this classic salad.

MAKE THE DRESSING

In a bowl, combine the ranch dressing, blue cheese, chives, sherry vinegar, Worcestershire sauce, and chopped pickles and mix well.

ASSEMBLE THE WEDGE SALAD

Place the wedges of lettuce on a plate and add the tomatoes around them. Season the lettuce and tomatoes with olive oil, lemon juice, and salt. Top with the bacon, the dressing, black pepper, and chives.

Ingredients

For the dressing:

- ½ cup (120 ml) Grillo's Ranch (page 201)
- ¼ cup (35 g) crumbled blue cheese
- 2 tablespoons minced fresh chives
- 1 tablespoon sherry vinegar
- 1 teaspoon Worcestershire sauce
- ½ cup (140 g) chopped Grillo's pickles

For the wedge salad:

- 1 head iceberg lettuce (about 1 pound/455 g), quartered
- ½ cup (90 g) sliced cherry tomatoes
- 1 tablespoon olive oil
- 1 tablespoon fresh lemon juice
- Salt and freshly ground black pepper
- 8 slices bacon, cooked and crumbled
- 2 tablespoons minced fresh chives

BISCUITS *with* PIMENTO CHEESE

Serves 4

Classic, Southern, flaky, delicious. Buttermilk and pickle brine make the perfect pair in these pickle biscuits.

Ingredients

- 2½ cups (315 g) plus 2 tablespoons all-purpose flour, plus more for dusting
- 2 tablespoons baking powder
- 1 tablespoon baking soda
- Salt
- 1 stick (4 ounces/115 g) very cold butter, small dice
- 1 cup (240 ml) buttermilk
- 3 tablespoons Grillo's pickle brine
- 3 tablespoons honey
- ½ cup (140 g) chopped Grillo's pickles
- 2 cups (480 g) Pimento Cheese Spread (page 200)
- ½ stick (2 ounces/55 g) butter, melted, for brushing

Preheat the oven to 425°F (220°C). Line a sheet pan with parchment paper.

In a medium bowl, combine the flour, baking powder, baking soda, and 1 teaspoon salt. Sift into a large bowl. Add the cold butter into the dry ingredients and mix until the butter is incorporated.

In a separate bowl, combine the buttermilk, pickle brine, 2 tablespoons of the honey, the chopped pickles, and pimento cheese.

Slowly incorporate the flour mixture into the wet ingredients, mixing as you go, until a wet dough is formed. Dust a cold surface (preferably marble) with flour and minimally work the dough into a ball, adding more flour to keep dough from sticking and getting too hot. Brush a wooden rolling pin with flour and roll the dough to a 1-inch (2.5 cm) thickness. With a 2-inch (5 cm) ring cutter, cut out 8 round biscuits and lay them on the lined sheet pan.

In a small bowl, combine the melted butter and remaining 1 tablespoon honey and brush over the biscuits. Finish with a pinch of salt.

Bake the biscuits until they have risen and are golden brown, about 12 minutes. Let cool on a rack. Serve with pimento cheese spread.

DILLY DEVILISH EGGS *with* RÉMOULADE

Serves 4

You dirty devil! A party isn't quite the same without an awesome deviled eggs recipe. This recipe even includes a family secret to add an extra layer of crunch!

Ingredients

- 1 teaspoon cornstarch
- 1 teaspoon baking powder
- Salt and freshly ground black pepper
- 8 ounces (225 g) store-bought chicken skin
- 8 large eggs
- 1½ cups (360 ml) Rémoulade (recipe follows)
- 1 (15-ounce/473 ml) container Grillo's spicy dill pickle chips
- Paprika
- Chopped chives

Preheat the oven to 350°F (180°C). Line a baking sheet with parchment paper.

In a bowl, stir together the cornstarch, baking powder, and salt and pepper to taste. Coat the chicken skin with this mixture. Lay the skin out on the lined baking sheet. Top with another sheet of parchment paper and another baking sheet.

Bake for 30 minutes. Uncover and bake until the skin is flat, golden brown, and very crispy, another 30 minutes.

Meanwhile, set up a bowl of ice and water. In a large pot, bring at least 4 cups (950 ml) water to a boil and turn the heat off. Add in the eggs and let them sit covered for 10 minutes, then transfer to the ice bath. Once cooled down, halve the eggs lengthwise and separate the yolks and whites.

In a bowl, mix the yolks and rémoulade into a smooth paste. Put the mixture in a piping bag and fill the egg whites. Place an egg white on a pickle chip and garnish with paprika, chopped chives, and a piece of crispy chicken skin.

(recipe continued)

RÉMOULADE

Makes 2 cups (235 g)

In a bowl, stir together the mayo, cooked yolks, chopped pickles, garlic powder, mustard, smoked paprika, black pepper, salt, and cayenne. Store in fridge for up to 2 weeks.

Ingredients

- 1 cup (240 ml) Duke's mayo
- 8 hard-boiled egg yolks, smashed into a paste
- ½ cup (140 g) chopped Grillo's spicy dill pickle chips (120 ml)
- 1 tablespoon garlic powder
- 1 tablespoon store-bought coarse ground mustard
- 1 tablespoon smoked paprika
- 1 tablespoon freshly ground black pepper
- 1 tablespoon salt
- 1 teaspoon cayenne pepper

BRIGHT AND BRINY GAZPACHO

Serves 4

Perfect for hot summer nights. While a cold soup may not make a lot of sense to some, one taste of this refreshing gazpacho will change their minds forever.

Measure out 1 tablespoon each of the yogurt and chopped pickles and set aside for garnish.

In a blender, combine the remaining yogurt and pickles, the pickle brine, sour cream, olive oil, cucumber, garlic, shallot, bell pepper, cilantro, dill, and white pepper. Blend on high until smooth. If you'd like the gazpacho thinner, add a little water or more oil. Season with salt to taste.

Serve garnished with the reserved yogurt and chopped pickles and fresh dill sprigs.

Ingredients

- 1 cup (240 ml) Greek yogurt
- ¼ cup (70 g) chopped Grillo's hot dill pickles
- ¼ cup (60 ml) Grillo's spicy pickle brine
- ¼ cup (60 ml) sour cream
- 1 tablespoon olive oil, plus more as needed
- ½ cup (65 g) peeled, deseeded, chopped cucumber
- 1 garlic clove, minced
- 1 tablespoon diced shallot
- ½ cup (75 g) chopped green bell pepper
- ½ cup (20 g) chopped fresh cilantro
- ½ cup (25 g) chopped fresh dill
- ¼ teaspoon ground white pepper
- Salt
- Small sprigs fresh dill, for garnish

STUFFED PICKLED POPPERS

Serves 4

Jalapeños are so last summer. While this recipe should theoretically feed four, you might want to double up on account of how delicious these poppers are. You can also change this recipe up by putting them on the grill!

PRO TIP: *Soak the skewers in water first so they don't burn.*

Pour 6 inches (15 cm) oil into a dutch oven or deep heavy pot. Heat the oil to 350°F (177°C).

In a bowl, combine the cream cheese, Cheddar, chopped pickles, scallions, cayenne, garlic powder, and paprika and stir to blend. Season it with salt and pepper to taste. Fill the cored and halved pickles with the mixture and wrap each with 2 slices of bacon. Pierce the poppers with skewers on either end like a goal post.

Fry the poppers until crispy, with the ends of the skewers facing up and out of the oil. Serve with ranch dressing.

Ingredients

- Vegetable oil, for deep-frying
- 4 ounces (115 g) cream cheese, at room temperature
- 1 cup (115 g) shredded Cheddar cheese
- ½ cup (140 g) chopped Grillo's pickles
- ½ cup (50 g) chopped scallions
- 1 teaspoon cayenne pepper
- 1 teaspoon garlic powder
- 1 teaspoon paprika
- Salt and freshly ground black pepper
- 4 Grillo's whole kosher dill pickles, halved lengthwise and cored (to make boats)
- 8 slices bacon
- 8 medium wooden skewers
- ½ cup (120 ml) Grillo's Ranch (page 201)

SALMON TARTARE

Serves 4

Say ta-ta to boring tartare. Brush up on your knife skills because this recipe is all about dicing.

In a medium bowl, combine the chopped pickles, shallot, chives, olive oil, Dijon mustard, pickled mustard seeds, and mayonnaise and mix well. Fold in the salmon. Salt to taste. Garnish with more chives and serve with toasted bread.

Ingredients

½ cup (140 g) chopped Grillo's pickles

1 shallot (25 g), minced

¼ cup (11 g) minced fresh chives, plus more for garnish

2 tablespoons olive oil

1 tablespoon Dijon mustard

1 tablespoon Pickled Mustard Seeds (page 26)

1 tablespoon mayonnaise

5 ounces (150 g) fresh salmon, diced (1 cup)

Salt

Toasted bread, for serving

DILL-AMATIC BAGELS *and* CREAM CHEESE

Serves 4

There's nothing quite like a fresh toasted bagel. This bagel is the perfect way to start or end your day and if you're feeling really crazy you could even eat it for lunch.

PRO TIP: *Add some lox and pickles into the mix to make a sandwich and it's game over.*

Measure out 1 tablespoon each of the dill and chives and set aside for garnish.

In a small bowl, combine the cream cheese, remaining herbs, chopped pickles, and salt and pepper to taste.

Construct open-face sandwiches by layering a generous spread of the cream cheese mixture onto the toasted bagels. Garnish with the reserved herbs.

Ingredients

¼ cup (13 g) chopped fresh dill

¼ cup (11 g) minced fresh chives

4 ounces (115 g) cream cheese

¼ cup (70 g) chopped Grillo's pickles

Salt and freshly ground black pepper

4 everything bagels, split and lightly toasted

FLUKE CEVICHE *with* PICKLE AGUACHILE

Serves 4

Did she say ceviche? This ceviche is perfect for date nights or dinner parties and will have everyone begging for the recipe.

MAKE THE PICKLE AGUACHILE

In a blender, combine half of the pickles, the cilantro, lime juice, pickle brine, sugar, jalapeño, cucumber, garlic, olive oil, and salt to taste. Blend on high until the aguachile is smooth.

MAKE THE FLUKE CEVICHE

In a small bowl, combine the fluke, chives, shallots, and lime juice. Season with salt.

To serve, spoon the ceviche into a shallow bowl and spread a generous amount of the aguachile around it. Garnish with dill and the remaining pickles.

Ingredients

For the pickle aguachile:

½ cup (140 g) chopped Grillo's pickles

½ cup (20 g) chopped fresh cilantro

2 tablespoons fresh lime juice

2 tablespoons Grillo's pickle brine

1 teaspoon sugar

⅓ jalapeño, chopped

½ Persian (mini) cucumber, chopped

1 garlic clove, minced

2 tablespoons olive oil

Salt

For the fluke ceviche:

5½ ounces (150 g) fluke fillet, diced (about 1 cup)

¼ cup (11 g) minced fresh chives

1 shallot, small diced

1 tablespoon fresh lime juice

Salt

Fresh dill

DRESSED UP OYSTERS *with* PICKLE MIGNONETTE

Serves 4

All dressed up with nowhere to go. No plans? No problem. Build your own shellfish tower at home and top your favorite oysters with our Pickle de Gallo mignonette.

Ingredients

- ½ cup (120 g) Grillo's Pickle de Gallo
- 2 tablespoons Grillo's pickle brine
- 2 tablespoons sherry vinegar
- 2 tablespoons fresh lemon juice
- ¼ cup (30 g) minced shallots
- ¼ cup (11 g) minced fresh chives
- Salt
- 24 oysters (your choice)
- Crushed ice

In a small bowl, combine the Pickle de Gallo, pickle brine, vinegar, lemon juice, shallots, and chives. Season with salt to taste.

Set an oyster belly side down (flat side up) on a folded towel. If you're right-handed, position the oyster so that its hinge (where the shells taper together) is pointing to the right; if you're a lefty, you'll want to point that hinge to the left.

Now fold the towel over the oyster so that only the hinge is exposed and place your nondominant hand on top to hold it steady. Work your oyster knife into the hinge. Wiggle the knife around until you feel like you can exert some pressure against both the top and bottom shells at once by twisting and prying the knife.

Work the oyster knife up and down, while also twisting and rotating it until you hear a "pop." Once the shells have popped, twist your knife so that the broad flat of the blade pries the shells apart even more. Cut the muscle until you can separate the top of the shell from the bottom. Throw the top shell away. You did it!

To serve, place the shucked oysters over a bed of crushed ice and top with pickle mignonette.

Dressed Up Oysters
with Pickle Mignonette
(page 73)

Fluke Ceviche with
Pickle Aguachile
(page 72)

BRAISED BEANS *with* CHARRED PICKLES

Serves 4

Beans just got a whole new look, and we're loving it. These beans get a 12-hour bath, but they're worth it in the end. Maybe you should think about taking a bath, too, while you're waiting.

MAKE THE BRAISED BEANS

Soak the black beans in 2 quarts (2 L) water for 12 hours. Drain well.

In a medium soup pot, heat 2 tablespoons of the oil over medium heat. Add the garlic, onion, and jalapeño and cook until soft and aromatic, about 10 minutes. Add the adobo seasoning, cayenne, coriander, garlic powder, onion powder, and paprika and cook until fragrant, about 5 minutes.

Add the chicken stock, 4 cups (960 ml) water, and the pickle brine and bring to a simmer. Add the soaked beans and cook until the beans are tender, about 1 hour.

Remove the beans from the heat and season with the ketchup, brown sugar, vinegar, and salt and pepper to taste.

When ready to serve, preheat a cast-iron skillet over high heat.

(recipe continued)

Ingredients

For the braised beans:

- 2 cups (370 g) dried black beans
- 6 tablespoons (90 ml) vegetable oil
- ¼ cup (35 g) chopped garlic
- ¼ cup (35 g) finely diced onion
- ¼ cup (40 g) finely diced jalapeño
- 1 tablespoon adobo seasoning
- 1 teaspoon cayenne pepper
- 1 teaspoon ground coriander
- 1 teaspoon garlic powder
- 1 teaspoon onion powder
- 1 teaspoon paprika
- 4 cups (960 ml) chicken stock
- 1 cup (240 ml) Grillo's pickle brine
- 2 tablespoons ketchup
- 2 tablespoons brown sugar

Add the remaining 4 tablespoons (60 ml) oil and heat until smoking. Sear the pickle spears for 2 minutes on each side. The pickles should be golden brown in color. Once done, chop into 1-inch (2.5 cm) pieces.

While the beans are still hot, stir in the pickle butter. Serve topped with the charred pickles.

1 tablespoon apple cider vinegar

Salt and freshly ground black pepper

8 Grillo's pickle spears, for serving

2 tablespoons Pickle Herb Butter (page 206), for serving

PICKLE PERFECT FLATBREAD

Serves 4

There's no need for store-bought flatbreads with this easy flatbread recipe. After resting the dough, you'll have tasty homemade flatbreads in minutes.

In a large bowl, combine the flour, yogurt, and chopped pickles and mix with a wooden spoon until all the ingredients are combined. Transfer the dough to a lightly floured surface and knead until smooth. Divide the dough into 4 equal balls. Cover and let rest at room temperature for 20 minutes.

When ready to cook, preheat a cast-iron griddle over medium heat. Roll out each ball of dough to a round ¼ inch (6 mm) thick and brush both sides of the round with the herb butter. Heat the oil in your pan and then char the flatbread for 2 minutes on each side or until golden brown. Finish with more herb butter and enjoy.

Ingredients

- 2½ cups (315 g) self-rising flour, plus more for dusting
- 1 cup (240 ml) whole-milk yogurt
- ¼ cup (70 g) chopped Grillo's pickles
- 2 tablespoons Pickle Herb Butter (page 206)
- 2 tablespoons vegetable oil

PICKLE HOUSE ROLLS

Makes 16 rolls

An homage to Boston's iconic Parker House Hotel. Light and airy, you'll be wanting baskets on baskets of these delicious pickle rolls.

In a stand mixer fitted with the dough hook, combine the flour, yeast, sugar, salt, mashed potatoes, milk, chopped pickles, room-temperature butter, and egg and mix for 10 minutes on medium speed. Transfer the dough to a lightly greased bowl, cover, and set aside until doubled in size, about 1 hour.

Line a baking sheet with parchment paper. Turn the dough out onto a work surface, punch down the dough, and divide into 16 equal portions. Roll into balls and lay each bun on the lined baking sheet, cover, and let rise until doubled in size, about 1 hour.

About 30 minutes before the rolls are risen, preheat the oven to 350°F (180°C).

Brush each bun with melted butter and top with a light layer of finishing salt.

Bake the rolls until golden brown and fluffy, about 16 minutes. Let cool on a rack.

Ingredients

4 cups (500 g) all-purpose flour

2 ½ teaspoons dry active yeast

2 tablespoons plus 2 teaspoons (33 g) sugar

2½ teaspoons salt

1 cup (210 g) mashed potatoes (do not add any milk or butter)

1 cup (240 ml) milk

½ cup (140 g) chopped Grillo's pickles

1 stick (4 ounces/115 g) butter, at room temperature

1 large egg

2 tablespoons (1 ounce/28 g) butter, melted, for brushing

1 tablespoon finishing salt

BANGIN' BENEDICT

Serves 4

Who says you can't have pickles for breakfast? This homemade hollandaise sauce gets its zing from pickle brine—it's so good you'll want seconds.

MAKE THE HOLLANDAISE SAUCE

In a medium saucepan, bring 4 cups (960 ml) water to a bare simmer. In a heat-resistant medium bowl, vigorously whisk the egg yolks and pickle brine until thickened and doubled in volume. Place the bowl over the saucepan. Slowly drizzle in the clarified butter, continuing to whisk until the mixture has the consistency of a creamy sauce. Add the Pickle de Gallo and season with cayenne and salt. Cover and store in a warm place.

MAKE THE EGGS BENEDICT

In a medium pot, bring 1 quart (1 L) water to a simmer with the distilled vinegar. Working in 2 batches of 4 eggs each, poach the eggs: Crack an egg into a small dish and gently slide the egg into the simmering water. Continue in the same manner for the remaining eggs. Stir with a wooden spoon until a vortex is formed. Poach for 3 minutes. Remove with a slotted spoon and set on a paper towel to drain.

Preheat a griddle to medium-high heat. Add the butter to the griddle and sear the ham with a grill press until crispy on both sides, about 4 minutes.

On each English muffin half, layer ham, egg, and hollandaise and enjoy.

Ingredients

For the hollandaise sauce:

4 large egg yolks

1 tablespoon Grillo's pickle brine

½ cup (120 ml) clarified butter

2 tablespoons Grillo's Pickle de Gallo

1 teaspoon cayenne pepper

Salt

For the eggs Benedict:

1 teaspoon distilled vinegar

8 large eggs

½ tablespoon butter

8 thick slices Taylor ham (or any ham you prefer)

4 English muffins, split and toasted

SAM SAM'S

FUN FACT

DID YOU KNOW THAT GRILLO'S PICKLES WAS STARTED OUT OF A WOODEN PICKLE CART SELLING 2 SPEARS FOR $1 ON THE STREETS OF BOSTON AT THE PARK STREET T STOP? THE ORIGINAL GRAB-AND-GO PICKLE!

Chapter 4

ALL THINGS FRIED

Frying food is basically a cheat code. Some would say everything is better fried . . . while we can't get behind that 100 percent, we can guarantee that this next chapter is filled with mouthwatering recipes that will keep that pan sizzling.

So, stock up on napkins, wet wipes, and maybe even a bib, and get ready to dive into our favorite fried recipes that will satisfy your fast-food cravings.

COOL AS A CUCUMBER CUBANO BITES

Serves 4

These yummy Cubano bites will have you salsa dancing around the dinner table. Two types of cheese, braised pork shoulder, and deli ham are just the beginning when it comes to this recipe.

In a medium bowl, mix the pulled pork, ham, mozzarella, Swiss cheese, yellow mustard, and chopped pickles. Refrigerate for 1 hour.

Divide the mixture into ¼-cup (55 g) portions and roll in panko until fully coated. Refrigerate for 1 hour.

Pour 6 inches (15 cm) oil into a deep heavy pot and heat the oil to 350°F (177°C).

Working in batches to avoid crowding, add the Cubano bites and fry until golden brown and crispy, about 5 minutes. Season the outside with salt and pepper to taste. Serve with yellow mustard and a pickle chip and enjoy.

(recipe continued)

Ingredients

2 cups (300 g) pulled Braised Pork Shoulder (recipe follows)

1 cup (130 g) diced deli ham

½ cup (55 g) shredded mozzarella cheese

½ cup (55 g) shredded Swiss cheese

2 tablespoons yellow mustard, plus more for serving

1 cup (280 g) chopped Grillo's pickles, drained

2 cups (160 g) panko bread crumbs

Vegetable oil, for deep-frying

Salt and freshly ground black pepper

4 Grillo's pickle chips

BRAISED PORK SHOULDER

Makes 2 cups (300 g)

- 1 tablespoon adobo seasoning
- 1 tablespoon salt
- 1 teaspoon chipotle powder
- 1 teaspoon ground cumin
- 1 teaspoon dried oregano
- 1 teaspoon paprika
- 1 teaspoon freshly ground black pepper
- 8 garlic cloves, minced
- 2 tablespoons vegetable oil
- 2½ pounds (1.2 kg) boneless pork shoulder
- 2 cups (480 ml) orange soda
- 1 cup (240 ml) Grillo's pickle brine or Basic Brine (page 20)

Preheat the oven to 350°F (180°C).

In a small bowl, combine the adobo seasoning, salt, chipotle powder, cumin, oregano, paprika, black pepper, garlic, and oil. Massage this mixture into the pork shoulder until well coated.

Transfer the pork shoulder to a roasting pan, slide into the oven, and cook for 30 minutes uncovered.

Pour in the orange soda and pickle brine. Cover with a lid (or aluminum foil) and cook until the pork is very tender and almost falling apart, about 2½ hours.

Shred the pork and stir into the cooking juices in the roasting pan and let cool.

SOUTHERN FISH FRY

Serves 4

You can start your diet next week. Pickle-marinated cod stays juicy under a crispy, crunchy coating and is only made better with tangy pickle tartar sauce.

In an airtight container, cover the cod with the pickle brine and marinate in the refrigerator for 2 hours.

In a bowl, combine all but 2 tablespoons of the flour, the baking powder, and cornstarch and whisk until fully incorporated. Gradually whisk in the egg and the beer until a batter is formed.

Pour 6 inches (15 cm) oil into a deep pot and heat the oil to 350°F (177°C).

Lightly dust the fish in the reserved flour and dip in the batter until fully coated. Add to the hot oil and fry until golden brown and crispy, about 6 minutes. Season with salt.

Garnish with chopped chives and serve with the tartar sauce and french fries.

Ingredients

- 2 pounds (910 g) cod, cut into 4 portions
- ½ cup (120 ml) Grillo's pickle brine or Basic Brine (page 20)
- ¾ cup (95 g) all-purpose flour
- 1 tablespoon baking powder
- ½ cup (65 g) cornstarch
- 1 large egg, lightly beaten
- 2 cups (480 ml) beer
- Vegetable oil, for deep-frying
- Salt
- 1 tablespoon of chopped chives
- ¼ cup (60 ml) Pickle TIme Tartar Sauce (page 203)
- Store-bought frozen french fries, for serving (our favorite brand is Ore-Ida fries)

I RELISH THESE CRAB CAKES

Serves 4

There's no need to be crabby with these crispy crab cakes on the table. They are so easy to make and equally delicious.

PRO TIP: *If you really want to turn up the heat, top them off with Tabasco.*

Ingredients

- 1 pound (455 g) jumbo lump crabmeat, drained
- 1 cup (80 g) panko bread crumbs
- 1½ cups (360 ml) Rémoulade (page 64)
- 1 large egg
- Vegetable oil, for shallow-frying

In a bowl, combine the crabmeat, panko, 1 cup (240 ml) of the rémolaude, and the egg and stir. Form into ¼-cup (55 g) patties about 1-inch (2.5 cm) thick.

Pour 6 inches (15 cm) oil into a saucepan or skillet and heat to 350°F (177°C).

Add the crab cakes and fry until golden brown, about 6 minutes. Serve with the remaining ½ cup (120 ml) rémoulade.

CHEESEBURGER EGG ROLLS

Makes 12 egg rolls

These egg rolls are the perfect party favor with a crispy, crunchy shell and all the best ingredients of a cheeseburger. How can you go wrong?

Ingredients

- ¾ pounds (340 g) ground beef
- 1 tablespoon salted butter
- ½ cup (60 g) diced onion
- 1 teaspoon ground cumin
- 1 teaspoon salt
- 1 teaspoon onion powder
- 1 teaspoon paprika
- 1 teaspoon freshly ground black pepper
- 1 cup (115 g) shredded Cheddar cheese
- ¼ cup (60 ml) plus 2 tablespoons Grillo's Burger Sauce (page 206)
- ¼ cup (70 g) chopped Grillo's pickles
- Vegetable oil, for deep-frying
- 1 large egg, beaten
- 12 egg roll wrappers
- 2 tablespoons sesame seeds

Heat a large skillet over high heat. Add the beef and cook until golden brown and crispy, about 5 minutes. Set a sieve over a bowl and pour the contents of the skillet into the sieve. Transfer the beef to a large bowl and reserve the strained beef cooking fat separately. Add the butter and onion to the skillet and cook until the onion begins to caramelize, about 5 minutes. Add the cumin, salt, onion powder, paprika, and black pepper. Reduce the heat to low and cook for another 3 minutes so the spices become fragrant.

Add the onion to the bowl with the beef, along with the Cheddar, 2 tablespoons of the burger sauce, and the chopped pickles. Transfer the mixture to a refrigerator to chill for 1 hour.

Set a wire rack in a sheet pan near the stovetop. Pour 6 inches (15 cm) vegetable oil into a deep heavy pan and add the strained beef fat. Heat to 350°F (177°C).

Meanwhile, to assemble the egg rolls, set a small bowl with the beaten egg near your work surface. Lay an egg roll wrapper with a point facing you, like diamond, and add 2 tablespoons of filling. Fold the sides in, brush the top with beaten egg yolk, and roll very tightly. Repeat to make all 12 rolls.

(recipe continued)

Working in batches, fry the rolls in the hot oil, rotating them as they cook, until golden brown and crispy, about 5 minutes. Transfer to the wire rack and coat with a generous amount of sesame seeds as they are cooling.

Enjoy with the remaining ¼ cup (60 ml) burger sauce.

VEGAN NUGGETS *with* TAHINI GOCHUGARU DIP

Serves 6

For the vegan homies because vegans deserve a great nugget, too! Hearty lion's mane mushrooms take the place of meat in this nugget recipe. The textures and flavors pair well with the acidity and freshness that Grillo's pickles always bring to the table.

Ingredients

For the vegan nuggets:

2 pounds (910 g) lion's mane mushrooms, stems removed

½ cup (60 g) cashews

½ cup (125 g) cooked or canned chickpeas

5 garlic cloves

1 tablespoon soy sauce

1 cup (125 g) all-purpose flour

1 cup (130 g) cornstarch

1 tablespoon sugar

¼ cup (70 g) chopped Grillo's dill pickles, drained

1 (13.5- to 14-ounce/405 to 420 ml) can unsweetened cashew milk

4 cups (240 g) panko bread crumbs

MAKE THE VEGAN NUGGETS

Preheat the oven to 375°F (190°C).

Place the mushroom caps, cashews, chickpeas, and garlic cloves on a sheet pan. Roast until everything is a deep, golden brown, about 15 minutes. Transfer to a food processor and add the soy sauce, ⅔ cup (80 g) of the flour, the conrstarch, sugar, and dill pickles until smooth. Form them into bite-size nuggets (about 30 g each), set on a tray, and refrigerate for 30 minutes.

Set up a dredging station with three shallow bowls: Place the remaining ⅓ cup (40 g) flour in one, the cashew milk in the second, and the panko in the third. Dredge the nuggets first in the flour, then the cashew milk, then in the panko. Once they are all breaded, return them to the tray and place them in the fridge for 1 hour.

Cook the nuggets in an air fryer set to 400°F (205°C) for 15 minutes. Don't have an air fryer? You can deep-fry these in 6 inches (15 cm) of oil in a dutch oven heated to 350°F (177°C) and fry for 5 minutes or until golden brown.

(recipe continued)

MAKE THE TAHINI GOCHUGARU DIP

In a large bowl, whisk together the pickles, tahini, lime juice, gochujang, gochugaru, vinegar, and togarashi. Add the warm water a little at a time to thin it out if it's too thick.

Serve the crispy nuggets with the dip and enjoy!

For the tahini gochugaru dip:

½ cup (140 g) chopped Grillo's dill pickles, drained

½ cup (120 ml) tahini

2 tablespoons fresh lime juice

1 tablespoon gochujang

1 tablespoon gochugaru

1 tablespoon rice vinegar

1 tablespoon togarashi

¼ cup (60 ml) warm water (optional)

GRILLO'S PICKLES
FRESH
Pickle Spears
GRILLO'S PICKLES
GRILLO'S PICKLES
GRILLO'S PICKLES
GRILLO'S PICKLES
FRESH
Pickle Spears
GRILLO'S
GRILLO'S PICKLES
GRILLO'S PICKLES
GRILLO'S PICKLES

STUFFED CORN DOGS

Serves 6

These pickle corn dogs are sure to win first prize in your heart. Crunchy corn flakes make these extra crispy and extra delicious. Feel free to get creative with the toppings—I love to top them with crushed dill pickle potato chips!

MAKE THE BATTER

In a large bowl, whisk together ½ cup (60 g) flour, the cornflakes, cornmeal, paprika, onion powder, baking powder, and salt. In a separate bowl, combine the buttermilk, pickle brine, and egg and whisk until smooth. Slowly incorporate buttermilk mixture into cornmeal mixture while whisking. Cover and refrigerate for 30 minutes.

MAKE THE STUFFED CORN DOGS

Pour 6 inches (15 cm) vegetable oil into a dutch oven and heat the oil to 350°F (177°C).

With an apple corer, hollow out whole dill pickles and stuff hot dogs in the center of each pickle. Place a skewer in each. Ensure that the pickles are fully dry by patting with a paper towel, then dredge them in 2 tablespoons flour. Dip into the batter mixture and add to the hot oil. Fry in batches until golden brown and crispy, about 6 minutes.

Serve with yellow mustard if desired.

Ingredients

For the batter:

- All-purpose flour
- ½ cup (60 g) blended crumbled cornflakes (blend in a food processor until smooth)
- ½ cup (90 g) cornmeal
- 1 tablespoon paprika
- 1 tablespoon onion powder
- 1 tablespoon baking powder
- 1 tablespoon salt
- 1 cup (240 ml) buttermilk
- ½ cup (120 ml) Grillo's pickle brine
- 1 large egg

For the stuffed corn dogs:

- Vegetable oil, for deep-frying
- 6 Grillo's whole kosher pickles
- 6 hot dogs
- 6 extra-long wooden skewers
- All-purpose flour
- Mustard, for serving (optional)

FREAKISHLY GOOD FRIED PICKLES

Serves 4

Turn up your fried pickle recipe and impress even the most knowledgeable pickle connoisseurs. By allowing the pickles to dry out for about 1 hour before beginning the dredging process, you'll get a crunchy coating that won't slide off.

Ingredients

16 Grillo's pickle chips

1 cup (125g) all-purpose flour

1 cup (240 ml) buttermilk

1 tablespoon paprika

1 tablespoon garlic powder

1 teaspoon cayenne pepper

5 large eggs, beaten

1 (450 g) bag store-bought potato chips, crushed into a fine powder

Vegetable oil, for frying

Salt to taste

1 cup (240 ml) Grillo's Ranch (page 201)

Dry the pickle chips on a rack for about 1 hour.

Set up a dredging station with three shallow bowls: Spread the flour in one. Combine the buttermilk, paprika, garlic powder, cayenne, and beaten eggs in the second. And put the crushed potato chips in the third.

Set a wire rack in a sheet pan next to the stovetop. Pour 6 inches (15 cm) oil into a deep heavy pot and heat it to 400°F (205°C).

Dredge the pickles in the flour first, then the buttermilk, then the chips. Coat the pickles fully in potato chips to ensure an even crust. Fry in the oil until golden brown, about 5 minutes. Set on the rack to drain.

Salt to taste and serve with the ranch for dipping.

SAM SAM'S

FUN FACT

IF WE LIVED DURING THE TIME OF NAPOLEON WE'D TAKE HOME THE PRIZE!! DID YOU KNOW NAPOLEON WAS SUCH A BIG FAN OF PICKLES THAT HE PUT UP THE EQUIVALENT OF $250,000 AS A PRIZE TO WHOEVER COULD FIGURE OUT THE BEST WAY TO PICKLE AND PRESERVE FOODS FOR HIS TROOPS? NOW YOU KNOW— POWER TO THE PICKLE!

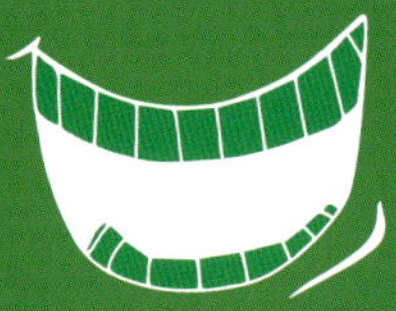

Chapter 5

SANDWICH LOVERS

A sandwich without a pickle just doesn't hit the same way. It's unfinished and weird, a mistake even.

We can all agree that there's really nothing better than stuffing your face with your favorite sandwich. A good sandwich is something that sticks with you your entire life. It can bring you back in time to your favorite childhood deli or remind you of that classic grilled cheese mom would make after school.

We hope these sandwiches become something to talk about for years to come with friends and family, just don't forget the pickles!

THE PICKLED BOY

Serves 4

Oh boy, we did it again! We can't promise that you won't get a little messy making this shrimp po'boy, but we *can* promise that it'll be worth it. Don't worry, no boys were hurt in the making of this recipe.

MAKE THE FRIED SHRIMP

Set up a dredging station with three shallow bowls. In the first bowl, mix together the flour, baking powder, onion powder, garlic powder, oregano, paprika, cayenne, and white pepper. In a second bowl, whisk the eggs with the pickle brine. Spread the cornmeal in the third.

Pour 6 inches (15 cm) vegetable oil into a dutch oven and heat to 350°F (177°C). Working in batches, dredge the shrimp in the flour, then the egg/pickle brine, and finish in the cornmeal. Drop the shrimp in the oil and fry until golden brown and crispy, about 4 minutes.

While the shrimp are frying, preheat the oven to 350°F (180°C).

(recipe continued)

Ingredients

For the fried shrimp:

- 1 cup (125 g) all-purpose flour
- 1 teaspoon baking powder
- 1 teaspoon onion powder
- 1 teaspoon garlic powder
- 1 teaspoon dried oregano
- 1 teaspoon paprika
- ½ teaspoon cayenne pepper
- ½ teaspoon ground white pepper
- 3 large eggs
- 2 tablespoons Grillo's pickle brine
- 1 cup (180 g) fine cornmeal
- Vegetable oil, for deep-frying
- 40 medium shrimp, peeled and deveined

ASSEMBLE THE PO'BOYS

Slice both of the French baguettes lengthwise, leaving hinged on one side, and then cut both in half. You will have 4 portions.

Preheat the oven to 350°F (180°C). Toast the buns open-face in the oven for 3 minutes.

Open the baguettes and spread a generous amount of rémoulade on both sides. Top with 10 shrimp, some lettuce, the tomatoes, and pickle chips.

For assembly of the po' boys:

- 2 (24-inch/61 cm) soft French baguettes
- ½ cup (120 ml) Rémoulade (page 64)
- 1 cup (75 g) shredded lettuce
- 8 slices tomatoes
- 1 (16-ounce/473 ml) container Grillo's Hot Dill Pickle Chips

FISH TACOS *with* CREMA AND CHIMICHURRI

Serves 4

You'll want to celebrate Taco Tuesday every day with these fish tacos on the menu. In this recipe, tilapia gets a pickle chimichurri marinade, with a special zing from the crema.

MAKE THE CREMA

In a tall container (or the immersion blender cup), combine the sour cream, lime juice, pickle brine, cilantro, and cumin and blend with an immersion blender until smooth. Season with salt to taste. Refrigerate until serving time.

PREPARE THE FISH

Toss the tilapia pieces with the chimichurri and refrigerate in an airtight container for 2 hours.

Pour 6 inches (15 cm) oil into a dutch oven and heat to 350°F (177°C).

In a bowl, combine ¾ cup (95 g) flour, the chipotle powder, garlic powder, onion powder, and paprika. Measure out 2 tablespoons of the seasoned flour and set aside. Slowly whisk the egg and beer into the remaining seasoned flour until a batter is formed.

Lightly dust the fish in the reserved seasoned flour and dip in the batter until fully coated. Working in batches, fry the fish until golden brown and crispy, about 5 minutes.

(recipe continued)

Ingredients

For the crema:

½ cup (120 ml) sour cream

2 tablespoons fresh lime juice

1 tablespoon Grillo's pickle brine

¼ cup (10 g) chopped fresh cilantro

1 teaspoon ground cumin

Salt

For the fish:

1 pound (455 g) tilapia, cut into long 2-ounce (55 g) portions

2 tablespoons Pickle Chimichurri (page 202)

Vegetable oil, for deep-frying

All-purpose flour

1 teaspoon chipotle powder

1 teaspoon garlic powder

1 teaspoon onion powder

1 teaspoon paprika

1 large egg, lightly beaten

1 (12-ounce/360 ml) bottle Mexican beer

ASSEMBLE THE TACOS

Season the fish with the Tajín and salt to taste. Lightly char the tortillas by placing them directly on the burner over low heat for a few seconds. Make sure to watch closely—they burn quickly!

Build the tacos by topping each charred tortilla with tilapia, shredded cabbage, crema, and hot sauce. Serve with lime wedges and enjoy.

For the tacos:

1 tablespoon Tajín seasoning

Salt

8 soft taco flour tortillas

½ cup (40 g) shredded cabbage

Mexican hot sauce

1 lime, cut into wedges, for garnish

RISE & BRINE PASTRAMI EGG AND CHEESE

Serves 4

We'll take two. They say breakfast is the most important meal of the day. After trying this pastrami egg and cheese you'll never want to start the day any other way.

Ingredients

- 2 tablespoons (1 ounce/ 28 g) butter
- 1 pound 5 ounces (595 g) pastrami, sliced ¼ inch (6 mm) thick
- ½ cup (120 ml) Grillo's pickle brine or Basic Brine (page 20)
- 8 slices American cheese
- 4 large eggs
- Salt and freshly ground black pepper
- 4 kaiser rolls, split and toasted
- Ketchup and hot sauce, for serving

In a large saucepan, melt 1 tablespoon of the butter over high heat. Add the pastrami and sauté until charred, about 5 minutes. Add the pickle brine, cover, and cook until the pastrami is tender and has absorbed all the liquid, about 5 minutes. Place the American cheese slices on top of the pastrami and cover again until the cheese is fully melted.

In a medium skillet, melt the remaining 1 tablespoon butter over medium heat. Add the eggs and cook sunny-side up, about 3 minutes. Season with salt and pepper.

To build the sandwich, cover the bottom half of a kaiser roll with a layer of cheese-topped pastrami, add a fried egg, and finish with the top half of the roll. Wrap in foil to steam the bread and allow all the ingredients to marry together. Serve with ketchup and hot sauce.

Rise & Brine Pastrami Egg and Cheese (page 107)

NASDAQ 12212.60
Purrfect Ev
What's News
Business & Finance
Regulators seized First Republic Bank and struck a deal to sell the bulk of its operations to JPMorgan Chase, heading off a chaotic collapse that threatened to reignite the recent banking crisis. A1, A8-9
◆ Federal Reserve officials are on track to increase interest rates again at their meeting this week while
DIMITRIOS KAMBOURIS/GETTY IMAGES FOR THE MET MUSEUM/VOGUE
CAT'S MEOW: Actor Jared Leto, with Anne Hathaway
Met Gala Monday dressed as Choupette, the late
Metropolitan Museum of Art. The Met is hostin
Yellen W
Defa
$776M
$688M
$536M

BROWN BUTTER LOBSTER ROLLS

Serves 4

From New England, with love. Bibs not included. Lobster rolls are a Boston staple, and these brown butter lobster rolls are sure to get your mouth watering.

Cook the butter in a saucepan over low heat for about 10 minutes until amber. Stir occasionally to prevent the butter from burning.

In a large steamer, bring 4 quarts (3.8 L) water to a boil. Meanwhile, fill a large bowl with cold water and ice to make an ice bath.

Add the lobsters to the steamer, cover, and cook for 11 minutes. Transfer to the ice bath to stop the cooking process. When cool enough to handle, take the meat out of the shells using a mallet or the back or a heavy knife. Chop the lobster meat into 1-inch (2.5 cm) pieces.

In a large bowl, combine the lobster meat, pickle mayo, brown butter, lemon juice, and chives. Season with salt.

Stuff the lobster mixture in the toasted brioche rolls. Top each roll with chives, a squeeze of lemon juice, and a pickle chip.

Ingredients

½ stick (2 ounces/55 g) butter

4 (2-pound/910 g) live lobsters

½ cup (120 ml) Pickle Mayo (page 200)

1 tablespoon fresh lemon juice, plus wedges for squeezing

¼ cup (11 g) minced fresh chives, plus more for garnish

Salt

4 split-top brioche rolls, toasted

4 Grillo's pickle chips

GRILLO'S
PICKLES

TUNA MELTS

Serves 4

A tuna melt to rival all other tuna melts . . . but we aren't biased or anything. Chopped pickles add a distinctive crunch and flavor to this epic sandwich.

In a medium bowl, combine the tuna, tartar sauce, lemon juice, red onion, ¼ cup (70 g) chopped pickles, and chives. Season with salt.

Preheat a griddle to medium heat.

For each sandwich, add a generous scoop of tuna salad to a slice of bread. Top with 2 slices of cheese and a second slice of bread. Melt 2 tablespoons butter (or as needed) on the griddle and cook the sandwich until golden brown on both sides and the cheese is melted, about 3 minutes per side. Open the sandwich and layer in potato chips, lettuce, tomatoes, and pickle chips. Cut the sandwich on a diagonal and enjoy.

Ingredients

2 cans tuna, drained (about 10 ounces/280 g total)

¼ cup (60 ml) Pickle Time Tartar Sauce (page 203)

1 tablespoon fresh lemon juice

¼ cup (35 g) minced red onion

¼ cup (70 g) chopped Grillo's pickles

¼ cup (11 g) minced fresh chives

Salt

8 thick-cut slices sandwich bread

8 slices Swiss cheese

8 tablespoons (4 ounces/115 g) butter

Your favorite store-bought potato chips

Shredded lettuce

Sliced tomatoes

1 (16-ounce/473) container Grillo's dill pickle chips

CHICKEN AND WAFFLE SLIDERS

Serves 4

When you're mixing breakfast, lunch, and dinner, what could go wrong? There's no bad time to eat this classic slider. Except maybe when you're in the shower.

MAKE THE SPICE BLEND

In a medium bowl, combine the paprika, cayenne, garlic powder, chipotle powder, brown sugar, and MSG.

PREPARE THE CHICKEN

In an airtight container, pour the brine over chicken thighs and refrigerate for 12 hours.

Rinse the chicken and place in another airtight container. In a medium bowl, whisk together the buttermilk, hot sauce, egg, salt and black pepper to taste, and 2 tablespoons flour. Pour the mixture over the chicken and marinate in the refrigerator for 12 hours.

In a medium bowl, combine 2 cups (250 g) flour, the cornstarch, and spice blend. Dredge the chicken in the flour mixture until fully coated and let sit for 1 hour so that the flour adheres.

Set a wire rack in a sheet pan next to the stovetop.

(recipe continued)

Ingredients

For the spice blend:

2 tablespoons paprika

2 teaspoons cayenne pepper

2 teaspoons garlic powder

2 tablespoons chipotle powder

2 tablespoons brown sugar

1 teaspoon MSG

For the chicken:

2 boneless, skinless chicken thighs, quartered

1 cup (240 ml) Grillo's Chicken Brine (page 23)

1 cup (235 g) buttermilk

1 tablespoon hot sauce

1 large egg

Salt and freshly ground black pepper

All-purpose flour

½ cup (65 g) cornstarch

Vegetable oil, for deep-frying

Pour 6 inches (15 cm) oil into a dutch oven and heat to 350°F (177°C). Add the chicken and fry for 6 minutes. Set the chicken on the wire rack. Increase the oil temperature to 375°F (190°C) and fry the chicken a second time until golden brown and very crispy, about 2 minutes.

MAKE THE SLIDERS

In a cup with a pour spout, stir together the honey, pickle brine, and chipotle powder. Drizzle the mixture over the chicken.

Use 2 waffles per slider and layer on the chicken and pickle chips.

For the sliders:

¼ cup (60 ml) honey

1 tablespoon Grillo's pickle brine

2 teaspoons chipotle powder

16 frozen mini waffles, heated in a toaster

1 (16-ounce/437 ml) container Grillo's dill pickle chips

BLT-P

Serves 4

**'Cause what's a BLT without the P?
The only other letter that could make this sandwich better.**

In a skillet over medium heat, add the bacon and cook for 2 minutes until crispy. Set aside to drain.

Build each sandwich by slathering the toast with the mayo and layering on the bacon, tomato, lettuce, and pickles. Enjoy.

Ingredients

- 1 pound (455 g) thin sliced bacon
- 8 thick-cut slices sandwich bread, toasted
- ½ cup (120 ml) Best Pickle Mayo (page 200)
- 8 thick slices tomato
- Shredded lettuce
- 16 Grillo's dill pickle chips

PICKLEVILLE HOT CHICKEN

Serves 4

Hotter than your average. Why waste your money on a flight to Nashville when you can make this hot chicken recipe at home?

PRO TIP: *Don't skip the MSG.*

MAKE THE NASHVILLE HOT SPICE BLEND

In a medium bowl, combine the brown sugar, black pepper, paprika, cayenne, chipotle powder, garlic powder, and MSG. Divide the spice blend in half.

MAKE THE SPICY CHICKEN FAT

In a saucepan, heat the chicken fat to 325°F (163°C). Place one-half of the spice blend in a heatproof bowl. Pour the hot chicken fat into the spice blend, whisking constantly. Store in an airtight container in the refrigerator.

(recipe continued)

Ingredients

For the Nashville hot spice blend:

- 2 tablespoons brown sugar
- 1 teaspoon freshly ground black pepper
- 2 tablespoons paprika
- 2 teaspoons cayenne pepper
- 2 teaspoons chipotle powder
- 2 teaspoons garlic powder
- 2 teaspoons MSG

For the spicy chicken fat:

- ½ cup (105 g) chicken fat

For the chicken:

1 cup (240 ml) Grillo's Chicken Brine (page 23)

4 boneless, skinless chicken thighs

1 cup (240 ml) buttermilk

1 tablespoon hot sauce

1 large egg

2 teaspoons salt

1 teaspoon freshly ground black pepper

2 cups (250 g) plus 2 tablespoons all-purpose flour

½ cup (65 g) cornstarch

Vegetable oil, for deep-frying

For assembly of the sandwiches:

2 tablespoons (1 ounce/ 28 g) butter

4 potato buns, split

½ cup (120 ml) Grillo's Ranch (page 201)

16 Grillo's pickle chips

PREPARE THE CHICKEN

In an airtight container, pour the brine over the chicken thighs and refrigerate for 12 hours.

Rinse the chicken. In a bowl, whisk together the buttermilk, hot sauce, egg, salt, black pepper, and 2 tablespoons of the flour. Store the chicken in an airtight container for 12 hours.

In a bowl, combine the remaining 2 cups (250 g) flour, the cornstarch, and remaining spice blend. Dredge the chicken in the flour until fully coated and let sit for 1 hour in the fridge so that the flour adheres.

Set a wire rack in a sheet pan next to the stovetop. Pour 6 inches (15 cm) oil into a dutch oven and heat to 350°F (177°C).

Add the chicken and fry for 6 minutes. Transfer to the wire rack. Increase the oil temperature to 375°F (190°C) and fry chicken a second time until golden brown and very crispy, about 2 minutes. Brush with a generous amount of spicy chicken fat.

ASSEMBLE THE SANDWICHES

Preheat a cast-iron skillet over medium heat. Melt the butter and toast the buns in butter on both sides until golden brown. Top each with a piece of fried chicken, 2 tablespoons of ranch dressing, and 4 slices of Grillo's pickles.

Pickleville Hot Chicken (page 118)

VEGGIE GG

Serves 4

Ripe avocado, fresh bell pepper, and crunchy jalapeño are just the beginning with this mouth-watering sandwich that makes lunch meat out of every other veggie sandwich you've ever had.

Among 4 slices of toast, divide evenly the smashed avocado, tomato slices, red bell pepper, jalapeño, arugula, Pickle de Gallo, pickle chips, and a generous drizzle of the green goddess dressing. Top with the remaining slices of toast. Add salt and pepper to taste.

Ingredients

- 8 slices thick-cut sandwich bread, toasted
- ⅔ cup (160 g) smashed avocado
- 8 slices tomato
- ½ cup (45 g) sliced red bell pepper
- ¼ cup (25 g) sliced fresh jalapeño
- 2 cups (40 g) baby arugula
- ½ cup (120 g) Grillo's Pickle de Gallo
- 20 Grillo's dill pickle chips
- ½ cup (120 ml) Green Goddess Dressing (page 201)
- Salt and freshly ground black pepper

BANH MI

Serves 4

This is a Grillo's twist on the classic Vietnamese sandwich. Packed with fresh ingredients and bold flavors, this is a sandwich you don't want to miss.

PRO TIP: *The pickled carrot and daikon radish are often sold specifically to make banh mi.*

PREPARE THE PORK BELLY

Puncture the pork belly with a metal skewer all over the skin about 25 times. In a small bowl, stir together the olive oil, soy sauce, shallots, garlic, sugar, Chinese five-spice, white pepper, and salt to make a paste. Rub this all over the pork belly. Set a wire rack in a sheet pan. Transfer the pork to the rack and place in the refrigerator skin side up and uncovered for 12 hours.

Preheat the oven to 350°F (180°C).

Brush the pork with the vinegar and cover with foil. Bake for 1 hour.

Switch the oven to the broil on low and remove the foil from the pork. Brush one more time with vinegar and broil until the skin is very crispy and a deep golden brown, about 30 minutes. The internal temperature of the pork belly should be 160°F (71°C).

Cut the cooked pork belly into 1-inch (2.5 cm) slices.

(recipe continued)

Ingredients

For the pork belly:

2 pounds (910 g) pork belly with skin

2 tablespoons olive oil

3 tablespoons soy sauce

2 tablespoons shaved (on a Microplane) shallots

2 tablespoons shaved (on a Microplane) garlic

1 tablespoon sugar

1 teaspoon Chinese five-spice powder

1 teaspoon ground white pepper

1 teaspoon kosher salt

2 tablespoons rice wine cider vinegar

For assembly of the banh mi:

2 (24-inch/61 cm) soft French baguettes

4 tablespoons (60 ml) Best Pickle Mayo (page 200)

ASSEMBLE THE BANH MI

Cut off each end the French baguettes, then split lengthwise, and cut both in half. You will have 4 portions.

Open the baguettes face up and spread with a generous amount of mayo on both sides. Top each with 7 slices of pork belly, pickled carrot and radish, cilantro, jalapeño, cucumber, Sriracha, and pickle chips.

1 cup (225 g) store-bought pickled carrot and daikon radish

½ cup (10 g) fresh cilantro leaves

¼ cup (25 g) fresh sliced jalapeño

¼ cup (25 g) cucumber matchsticks

½ cup (120 ml) Sriracha

1 (16-ounce/473 ml) Grillo's hot dill pickle chips

SAM SAM'S

FUN FACT

THE UNITED STATES OF PICKLES. EACH STATE HAS ITS OWN SET OF LAWS AND IN CONNECTICUT, IN ORDER FOR A PICKLE TO OFFICIALLY BE CONSIDERED A PICKLE, IT MUST BOUNCE.

CRÍSP

Chapter 6

DON'T GRILL WITHOUT GRILLO'S

Picture this: It's 93°F (34°C) out, the smell of hot pavement and fresh cut grass fills the air. You hear kids laughing, splashing in the pool or running around spraying each other with the hose.

It's summertime and you're finally ready to invite the homies over for a cookout. "Who's bringing the Grillo's?" gets blasted out in the group text. Next thing you know, everyone brought the Grillo's because your friends are real ones.

The following recipes are for grillin' and chillin'. They're for making memories and sharing stories. Remember, don't grill without Grillo's!

THE GRILLO'S SMASH BURGER

Serves 4

This smash burger took years to perfect. The secret is the crispy cheese skirt that protects the potato roll from the sauce and juicy beef.

MAKE THE CARAMELIZED ONIONS

In a medium pot, heat the vegetable oil over low heat. Add the onions and cook until they are soft and are a deep golden-brown, about 1 hour. Add the sherry vinegar and brown sugar for the last 5 minutes. Season with salt to taste.

MAKE THE BURGERS

Divide the beef into 4 equal portions and roll into balls.

Preheat a cast-iron flattop griddle to medium heat. Smear butter on the buns and place them face down for 3 minutes to achieve a golden-brown crust. Set the buns aside.

Increase the heat under the griddle to high. Smash the balls of ground beef on the griddle to patties ¼ inch (6 mm) thick. Season both sides with salt. Cook the burgers until deeply caramelized and golden brown, 4 minutes. Take the burgers off the griddle and reduce the heat to medium.

(recipe continued)

Ingredients

For the caramelized onions:

- 2 tablespoons vegetable oil
- 2 pounds (910 g) onions, thinly sliced
- 2 tablespoons sherry vinegar
- 2 tablespoons brown sugar
- Salt

For the burgers:

- 1 pound (455 g) ground beef
- 2 tablespoons (1 ounce/28 g) butter
- 4 soft hamburger buns (preferably King's Hawaiian), split
- Salt
- 4 cups (460 g) shredded Cheddar cheese
- 4 tablespoons Grillo's Burger Sauce (page 206)
- 20 Grillo's spicy pickle chips

Make 4 piles of shredded cheese on the surface of the griddle and let crisp up for 3 minutes. Rest the buns, toasted-side down on the cheese as it's melting; this will adhere the cheese to the bun and steam it at the same time.

Lay a cooked burger inside each bun. Top with a tablespoon of the caramelized onions, 1 tablespoon of the burger sauce, and 5 spicy Grillo's pickle chips. Wrap in a greaseproof wax paper.

GRILLED CHICKEN THIGHS

Serves 4

Marinate on this for a minute. Okay, now you can eat it.

Pour the brine over the chicken thighs in an airtight container and marinate in the refrigerator for 12 hours.

Rinse the chicken and place in a clean airtight container with the green goddess dressing and hot paprika. Marinate in the refrigerator for at least 4 hours.

Preheat a grill to high. Grill the chicken for 5 minutes on each side until they reach an internal temperature of 170°F (77°C).

Serve garnished with the scallions.

Ingredients

1 cup (240 ml) Grillo's Chicken Brine (page 23)

4 boneless, skinless chicken thighs

½ cup (120 ml) Green Goddess Dressing (page 201)

1 tablespoon hot paprika

2 tablespoons finely sliced scallions

Fish and Shishito Pepper Skewers (page 135)
Pickle-Marinated Veggies (page 134)
Briny Tater Salad (page 35)

Pickle Perfect Flatbread (page 79)
Shrimp on the Barbie (page 137)
Pickle-Marinated Veggies (page 134)
Ain't No Thang but a Chicken Wang (page 147)

PICKLE-MARINATED VEGGIES

Serves 4

Pickling your homegrown veggies is a fun way to extend the shelf life of your fresh veggies, but have you tried grilling them? This recipe is quick, easy, and a great way to make eating veggies fun for the entire family. The Pickle de Gallo on top is the equivalent to a cherry in this situation.

Preheat a grill to high.

In a bowl, toss the vegetables with the pickle chimichurri and pickle brine. Let marinate for an hour. Grill in a grill basket for 8 minutes to develop a nice char. Finish with Pickle de Gallo, lime juice, and salt.

Ingredients

1 pound (455 g) your favorite vegetables (we especially love asparagus)

2 tablespoons Pickle Chimichurri (page 202)

1 tablespoon Grillo's pickle brine

¼ cup (60 ml) Pickle de Gallo

1 tablespoon fresh lime juice

1 tablespoon salt

FISH AND SHISHITO PEPPER SKEWERS

Serves 4

Who doesn't love dinner on a stick? This recipe will elevate any cookout with these savory green peppers that are perfect for both roasting and snacking.

In an airtight container, toss the fish and shishito peppers with the chimichurri and salt. Marinate in the refrigerator for 1 hour.

Preheat a grill to high.

On each skewer, alternate 2 pieces of halibut and 3 shishito peppers. Grill for 3 minutes on each side. Serve with lime wedges for squeezing.

Ingredients

1 pound (455 g) halibut, cut into 16 chunks

24 shishito peppers (240 g)

¼ cup (60 ml) Pickle Chimichurri (page 202)

1 tablespoon salt

8 wooden skewers—soaked in water (to prevent burning)

Lime wedges, for squeezing

SHRIMP ON THE BARBIE

Serves 4

An absolute must-have for your backyard barbecue. Sometimes all it takes are a few simple ingredients to round out a dish. The fresh and herby pickle chimichurri adds a liveliness to the grilled shrimp. Best cooked over an open flame and eaten alongside your friends and family. Mom, are you impressed?

In a bowl, toss the shrimp in the chimichurri and salt and marinate in the fridge for 30 minutes.

Preheat a grill to high.

Skewer 4 shrimp per skewer and grill for 3 minutes on each side until they turn pink. Serve with lime wedges.

Ingredients

24 medium shrimp (about ½ pound/225 g), peeled and deveined

½ cup (120 ml) Pickle Chimichurri (page 202)

1 tablespoon salt

6 extra-long wooden skewers—soaked in water (to prevent burning)

1 lime, cut into wedges, for garnish

PICKLES

STREET "SONORA DOGS"

Serves 4

Bring some Mexican heat to your grill! Packed with Grillo's Pickle de Gallo, bacon, and more, this dog really is man's best friend.

Ingredients

- Vegetable oil, for frying
- ½ cup (30 g) sliced onion
- ½ cup (50 g) sliced bell pepper
- 4 all-beef hot dogs
- 8 slices bacon
- 8 small wooden skewers—soaked in water (to prevent burning)
- 4 split-top hot dog buns
- ½ cup (80 g) mashed avocado
- 2 tablespoons chopped fresh jalapeño
- 2 tablespoons Best Pickle Mayo (page 200)
- ¼ cup (60 ml) Grillo's Hot Pickle de Gallo

In a skillet, heat 2 tablespoons oil over medium heat. Add the onion and bell pepper and sauté until they soften, about 10 minutes.

Preheat a grill to medium.

Wrap each hot dog in 2 slices of bacon and skewer on each end like a goal post. Grill over low heat for 10 minutes.

Grill the buns for 3 minutes.

Set a hot dog in a bun and top with avocado, jalapeño, pickle mayo, sautéed onions and peppers, and Pickle de Gallo.

THE PB&B HOT DOG

Serves 4

Hear us out, this is the hot dog that will make all your munchie dreams come true. A classic PB&J just got better with peanut butter, potato chips, and bacon. You're an adult, you can have whatever you want for dinner.

In a small bowl, combine the hot sauce and jam and set aside.

Pour 6 inches (15 cm) oil into a dutch oven and heat to 350°F (177°C).

Preheat a grill to medium.

Wrap each hot dog in 2 slices of bacon and skewer on each end like a goal post. Add to dutch oven and deep-fry for 2 minutes. Coat the bacon-wrapped hot dogs with the spicy strawberry sauce and grill for 5 minutes, constantly basting with more sauce.

Place the hot dog buns face down on the grill until they are lightly browned. Generously spread peanut butter on the grilled buns and top with chopped pickles and potato chips.

Ingredients

- 3 tablespoons hot sauce
- 2 tablespoons strawberry jam
- Vegetable oil, for deep-frying
- 4 all-beef hot dogs
- 8 slices bacon
- 8 small wooden skewers—soaked in water (to prevent burning)
- 4 split-top hot dog buns
- ¼ cup (60 ml) creamy peanut butter
- ¼ cup (70 g) chopped Grillo's pickles
- 2 cups (70 g) potato chips

CLASSIC CHICAGO DOGS

Serves 4

A hot snap and a fresh CRUNCH. BOW WOW, big dogs only! Chicago dog is the ultimate dog for summertime fun. If you want to be really authentic make sure your sport peppers are ACTUALLY from Chicago.

Preheat a grill to high.

In a small bowl, cover the onion in water and soak for 30 minutes. Drain and set aside.

Grill the hot dogs for 7 minutes, rotating occasionally until nice and charred.

Set a hot dog in a split-top bun and top each with some mustard, tomatoes, a pickle spear, diced onion, 2 sport peppers, green relish, and celery salt.

Ingredients

- 2 tablespoons diced onion
- 4 all-beef hot dogs
- 4 split-top poppy seed hot dog buns, steamed
- 4 tablespoons yellow mustard
- 4 slices tomato, cut into half-moons
- 4 Grillo's pickle spears
- 8 sport peppers (spicy)
- 4 tablespoons Green Relish (page 203)
- 1 tablespoon celery salt

The PB&B Hot Dog
(page 140)

Classic Chicago Dogs
(page 141)

STUFFED PORTOBELLO MUSHROOM BURGERS

Serves 4

This burger is possibly meatier and more delicious than beef. With key ingredients like a soft potato bun and crunchy Grillo's pickles, every bite is like a delicious cloud of flavor.

Ingredients

For the filling:

- ½ cup (55 g) shredded mozzarella cheese
- 2 tablespoons cream cheese
- 1 teaspoon garlic powder
- 1 teaspoon onion powder
- 1 teaspoon paprika
- ½ teaspoon cayenne pepper
- ¼ cup (70 g) chopped Grillo's hot dill pickles
- 1 teaspoon salt

For the portobellos:

- Vegetable oil, for deep-frying
- 4 large portobello mushrooms, cleaned and stemmed
- All-purpose flour
- 2 large eggs
- 2 tablespoons Grillo's spicy pickle brine
- ⅔ cup (55 g) panko bread crumbs
- Salt

MAKE THE FILLING

In a bowl, stir together the mozzarella, cream cheese, garlic powder, onion powder, paprika, cayenne, chopped pickles, and salt.

PREPARE THE PORTOBELLOS

Pour 6 inches (15 cm) oil into a dutch oven, and heat the oil to 350°F (177°C).

Stuff each portobello mushroom generously with the filling.

Set up a dredging station with three shallow bowls: ½ cup (65 g) flour in one, the whisked eggs and pickle brine in a second, and the panko in the third. Coat each mushroom first in the flour, then the egg, then the panko.

Add the mushrooms to the pan and cook until golden brown and crispy, about 6 minutes, and season with salt.

(recipe continued)

Build each burger by layering in the potato rolls with some of the burger sauce, the fried mushroom cap, lettuce, tomato, and pickles. Top with more burger sauce.

For the burgers:

4 potato rolls, split and toasted

½ cup (120 ml) Grillo's Burger Sauce (page 206)

1 cup (55 g) shredded lettuce

4 tomato slices

16 Grillo's dill pickle chips

AIN'T NO THANG BUT A CHICKEN WANG

Serves 4

The world record for most chicken wings eaten is 501 wings in 30 minutes . . . that's a lot of wings. These wings are so good you might break the record. Are you up for the challenge? We believe in you.

Ingredients

- 4 cups (950 ml) Grillo's pickle brine or Basic Brine (page 20)
- ¼ cup (10 g) dill fronds
- 2 pounds (910 g) chicken wings (20 wings)
- 1 cup (240 ml) Pickle BBQ Sauce (page 204)

In a saucepan, combine the pickle brine, 4 cups (950 ml) water, and the dill and bring to a boil. Remove from the heat and submerge the wings in the hot poaching liquid. Let sit for 20 minutes, tightly covered, then uncover and refrigerate for 1 hour.

Preheat a grill to high.

Drain the wings and toss them with half of the BBQ sauce. Grill for about 8 minutes on each side, basting constantly with the remaining BBQ sauce.

SAM SAM'S

FUN FACT

GRILLO'S PICKLES ARE MADE FROM A HUNDRED-YEAR-OLD GARDEN-FRESH RECIPE. WE USE GRAPE LEAVES TO HELP SLOW DOWN FERMENTATION AND KEEP THE PICKLES EXTRA CRUNCHY AND FRESH!

CRUNCHY

Chapter 7

THE MAIN ATTRACTION

Why do pickles never get a chance to shine? Why are they always just an addition and never the main character? No more! In this chapter you'll see how pickles can be the star ingredient for some of your favorite dishes. You'll also come to understand that pickles just make everything better . . . and if you don't think so you might have picked up the wrong book! It's surprising that something as simple as a cucumber marinated in vinegar can have such a huge impact on the flavor of a dish. That crisp dill crunch and salty brine is sure to elevate any dinner.

PORK BELLY *with* CHOW CHOW

Serves 4

It's time to chow down. This fresh pickled strawberry and corn chow chow and Grillo's BBQ sauce adds the perfect amount of flavor and texture to this melt-in-your-mouth pork belly.

MAKE THE CHOW CHOW

In a saucepan, combine the vinegar, brine, mustard powder, ground turmeric, all the whole spices, the pepper flakes, and bay leaf. Bring to a simmer and cook for 5 minutes. Add the corn, green tomatoes, pickles, onion, and strawberries and continue to simmer over low heat for another 20 minutes. Let cool and refrigerate in an airtight container for up to 6 weeks.

PREPARE THE PORK BELLY

Puncture the pork belly with a metal skewer all over the skin about 25 times. In a small bowl, stir together the olive oil, Chinese 5-spice, salt, and white pepper to make a paste. Rub this all over the pork belly. Set a wire rack in a sheet pan. Transfer the pork to the rack and place in the refrigerator skin side up and uncovered for 12 hours.

Preheat the oven to 350°F (180°C).

Brush the pork with the vinegar and cover with foil. Bake for 1 hour.

(recipe continued)

Ingredients

For the chow chow:

- 1 cup distilled white vinegar
- ½ cup (120 ml) Grillo's pickle brine
- ½ teaspoon mustard powder
- ½ teaspoon ground turmeric
- ½ teaspoon whole cloves
- ½ teaspoon mustard seeds
- ½ teaspoon black peppercorns
- Pinch of crushed red pepper flakes
- 1 bay leaf
- 2 cups (290 g) corn
- ½ cup (90 g) diced green tomatoes
- ½ cup (140 g) chopped Grillo's pickles
- ½ cup (65 g) finely diced onion
- ½ cup (85 g) finely diced strawberries

Switch the oven to the broil on low and remove the foil from the pork. Brush one more time with vinegar and broil until the skin is very crispy and a deep golden brown, about 30 minutes. The internal temperature of the pork belly should be 160°F (71°C).

Once the pork comes out of the oven, brush it with half of the BBQ sauce and allow to rest for 10 minutes before slicing.

Cut the pork belly into 1-inch (2.5 cm) slices and top with the remaining BBQ sauce and some chow chow.

For the pork belly:

2 pounds (910 g) pork belly with skin

2 tablespoons olive oil

1 teaspoon Chinese 5-spice powder

1 teaspoon kosher salt

1 teaspoon ground white pepper

2 tablespoons apple cider vinegar

½ cup (120 ml) Pickle BBQ Sauce (page 204)

DILL-LIGHTFUL STUFFED CABBAGE

Serves 4

Just like Babcia makes, but with pickle juice. Or maybe Babcia does make it with pickle juice? I don't know, she refuses to share her secret recipe!

MAKE THE SAUCE

In a medium saucepan, heat the oil over medium-low heat and sweat the onion and garlic until soft and translucent, about 10 minutes. Add the hot paprika and bay leaves, reduce the heat to low, and cook for an additional 3 minutes. Pour in the chicken stock and pickle brine and cook until reduced by half, about 15 minutes. Whisk in the ketchup and heavy cream and simmer for another 5 minutes.

MAKE THE FILLING AND ASSEMBLE THE STUFFED CABBAGE

Heat a sauté pan over high heat and add the ground beef. Sear the beef until it is browned and cooked through, about 5 minutes. Drain the fat out of the pan. Set the beef aside in the pan.

In a small bowl, stir together one-quarter of the sauce and the egg. Fold this mixture into the ground beef. Season with salt and pepper. Set the filling aside.

Bring a medium pot of water to a boil. Add the cabbage leaves and cook until soft and tender, about 3 minutes. Drain the cabbage.

(recipe continued)

Ingredients

For the sauce:

1 tablespoon olive oil

½ cup (75 g) finely diced onion

¼ cup (35 g) chopped garlic

1 tablespoon hot paprika

2 bay leaves

2 cups (480 ml) chicken stock

1 cup (240 ml) Grillo's pickle brine or Basic Brine (page 20)

½ cup (120 ml) ketchup

½ cup (120 ml) heavy cream

For the filling and assembly:

1 pound (455 g) ground beef

1 large egg

Salt and freshly ground black pepper

8 large cabbage leaves

Yogurt, for drizzling

Chopped dill and scallions, for garnish

Spoon about 2 tablespoons of the beef mixture onto each cabbage leaf. To close, bring one end of the cabbage leaf over the mixture, rolling and tucking in the ends to prevent the filling from falling out.

Place the cabbage rolls in a large skillet and pour the remaining sauce on top. Cover and bring to a boil over medium heat. Reduce the heat to low and simmer until soft and tender, about 40 minutes, stirring and basting with the liquid often.

Plate, drizzle with yogurt, garnish with dill and scallions, and enjoy.

PICKLE-BRINED SPATCHCOCKED CHICKEN

Serves 4

Are you brave enough to try a pickle-brined chicken instead of turkey this holiday season? This herby spatchcocked chicken stays juicy thanks to a 12-hour bath in that classic Grillo's brine you know and love. Cook a chicken, spare a turkey.

PRO TIP: *Ask your butcher to spatchcock the chicken for you to save some time.*

Truss the chicken and set in an airtight nonreactive container big enough to hold the chicken and the brine. Add the pickle brine and make sure the chicken is submerged. Cover and refrigerate for 12 hours.

In a bowl, mix together the thyme, sage, salt, garlic powder, oregano, onion powder, paprika, black pepper, cayenne, mustard, and olive oil. Remove the chicken from the brine and pat it dry with a paper towel. Rub the skin of the chicken liberally with the herb/spice paste.

Preheat the oven to 425°F (220°C) and place the chicken in a roasting pan. Cook for about 30 minutes, until the internal temperature is 180°F (82°C). Let the chicken rest for at least 10 minutes before carving.

Ingredients

- 1 whole chicken (4 pounds/1.8 kg)
- 10 cups Grillo's Chicken Brine (page 23)
- ¼ cup (11 g) chopped fresh thyme
- ¼ cup (9 g) chopped fresh sage
- 1½ tablespoons kosher salt
- 1½ tablespoons garlic powder
- 1 tablespoon dried oregano
- 1 tablespoon onion powder
- 1 tablespoon paprika
- 1 teaspoon freshly ground black pepper
- ½ teaspoon cayenne pepper
- 1 tablespoon Dijon mustard
- 1 tablespoon olive oil

PORK SCHNITZEL *with* PICKLE YOGURT

Serves 4

As fun to eat as it is to say, this easy recipe is great for any night of the week, especially if you're in the mood for some good old-fashioned comfort food as the weather gets colder. Or maybe you just need to be cheered up because your pickle jar is empty.

MAKE THE SCHNITZEL

Set up a dredging station with three shallow bowls: Put the flour in one. In the second, beat the eggs with the pickle brine. Place the panko in the third. Dredge the pork first in the flour, then the egg/pickle brine, and finish in the panko.

In a large skillet, heat 2 tablespoons of the oil and 1 tablespoon of the butter over medium-high heat. The pan should be well coated, so add more oil if needed. Let the pan heat up for a few minutes. Add 2 of the breaded cutlets to the pan and fry until golden brown and crispy, about 3 minutes per side. Remove the cutlets to a plate. Repeat with the remaining 2 schnitzels, adding at least 1 more table-spoon olive oil and the remaining 1 tablespoon butter to the pan for frying. Season with salt and pepper.

(recipe continued)

Ingredients

For the schnitzel:

- ¼ cup (30 g) all-purpose flour
- 1 large egg
- ½ cup (120 ml) Grillo's pickle brine
- 1 cup (80 g) panko bread crumbs
- 4 boneless pork chops, pounded to a 1/4-inch (6 mm) thickness
- 3 tablespoons olive oil, plus more if needed
- 2 tablespoons (1 ounce/ 28 g) butter
- Salt and freshly ground black pepper

MAKE THE PICKLE YOGURT

In a bowl, stir together the yogurt, pickles, dill, garlic, lemon juice, honey, cumin, and salt and pepper to taste until fully combined.

Serve the schnitzel with the pickle yogurt on the side.

For the pickle yogurt:

1 cup (240 ml) yogurt

½ cup (140 g) chopped Grillo's pickles

¼ cup (13 g) chopped fresh dill

1 garlic clove, minced

1 tablespoon fresh lemon juice

1 tablespoon honey

1 teaspoon ground cumin

Salt and freshly ground black pepper

PULLED PORK MAC AND CHEESE *with* PICKLE SLAW

Serves 4

MAC AND CHEESE DIET! MAC AND CHEESE DIET! MAC AND CHEESE DIET! We're gonna need a bigger plate . . .

Ingredients

- Salt
- 8 ounces (225 g) elbow macaroni
- ½ stick (2 ounces/55 g) butter
- ½ cup (65 g) finely diced onion
- ¼ cup (30 g) all-purpose flour
- 1 teaspoon freshly ground black pepper
- 1 teaspoon paprika
- 2 cups (480 ml) whole milk
- 2 cups (230 g) shredded Cheddar cheese
- 2 cups (220 g) shredded Gruyère cheese
- 1 cup (150 g) shredded Braised Pork Shoulder (page 87)
- 2 tablespoons Pickle BBQ Sauce (page 204)
- Pickle Slaw (recipe follows)

In a medium pot of boiling salted water, cook the pasta for 9 minutes. Drain and set aside.

Meanwhile, in a medium saucepan melt butter over medium-low heat. Add the onion and sauté until translucent, about 10 minutes. Sprinkle in the flour, black pepper, paprika, and 1 teaspoon salt and gently stir for 2 minutes. Pour in the milk and whisk until combined. Bring the sauce to a boil until it thickens, whisking constantly. Slowly whisk in 1½ cups (170 g) of each cheese, ½ cup (55 g) at a time.

Set the oven to low broil.

In a bowl, combine the pasta and cheese sauce and spoon into a broilerproof medium baking dish. Top with the remaining ½ cup (55 g) of each cheese.

Broil the mac and cheese until golden brown and crispy, about 5 minutes.

In a small saucepan, heat the pulled pork and BBQ sauce. Serve the mac and cheese with pulled pork and slaw alongside.

(recipe continued)

PICKLE SLAW

Makes 4 cups (900 g)

¼ cup (70 g) chopped Grillo's pickles

2 tablespoons Grillo's pickle brine

2 tablespoons mayonnaise

1 tablespoon sugar

Salt and freshly ground black pepper

2 cups (190 g) shredded cabbage

½ cup (55 g) grated carrots

In a medium bowl, stir together the chopped pickles, pickle brine, mayonnaise, sugar, and salt and pepper to taste. Add the cabbage and carrots and toss until well coated.

Pulled Pork Mac and Cheese with Pickle Slaw (page 158)

LEGALLY BRINED LAMB CHOPS

Serves 4

Why count sheep when you can count your lamb chops instead? Pickle chimichurri and fresh yogurt pair perfectly with the full flavor of this dish.

In a medium bowl, mix together ¼ cup (60 ml) of the chimichurri, the yogurt, and salt and pepper to taste. Add the lamb chops. Transfer the meat and marinade to a freezer bag and store in the refrigerator for 12 hours to fully marinate.

Preheat a grill to high.

Brush the chops with the olive oil and grill until the internal temperature is 140°F (60°C), about 3 minutes per side.

Place the scallions on the grill and grill until charred.

Serve the chops on a bed of yogurt, topped with the remaining chimichurri and the scallions, and enjoy.

Ingredients

- ½ cup (120 ml) Pickle Chimichurri (page 202)
- ½ cup (120 ml) whole-milk yogurt, plus 2 tablespoons for serving
- Salt and freshly ground black pepper
- 8 medium lamb rib chops
- 1 tablespoon olive oil
- 6 scallions

OLD-DILL SHRIMP AND GRITS

Serves 4

Shrimp and grits have a way of making you feel like you just got a hug from the South. This recipe incorporates fresh pickle juice to add a zap of flavor to a classic meal that always hits just right.

MAKE THE SHRIMP

In a skillet, heat the oil over high heat. Add the onion and garlic, season with salt and pepper, and cook until translucent, about 10 minutes. Add the tomato paste, cayenne, coriander, and paprika and cook for 5 minutes. Add the brandy and deglaze the pan, then add the lobster stock, pickle brine, tarragon, and bay leaves. Cook the sauce over low heat for 1 hour to reduce by half.

Remove the bay leaves. Add the heavy cream and reduce for an additional 10 minutes. Add the shrimp to the sauce in the last 5 minutes of cooking.

(recipe continued)

Ingredients

For the shrimp:

2 tablespoons vegetable oil

½ cup (40 g) finely diced onion

¼ cup (35 g) chopped garlic

Salt and freshly ground black pepper

2 tablespoons tomato paste

1 teaspoon cayenne pepper

1 teaspoon ground coriander

1 teaspoon paprika

2 tablespoons brandy

2 cups (480 ml) lobster stock

1 cup (240 ml) Grillo's pickle brine

1 sprig fresh tarragon

2 bay leaves

4 ounces heavy cream

1 pound (455 g) jumbo shrimp (16/20 count), peeled and deveined

MAKE THE GRITS

In a medium bowl, combine the milk, water, and salt. Set over medium-high heat and slowly whisk in the grits. Allow the mixture to come to a boil, which will take 3 to 5 minutes, whisking every minute or so. Once the mixture comes to a boil, reduce the heat to low so it simmers. Cook uncovered, whisking regularly, until the grits are very creamy and thickened, about 30 minutes. Stir in the butter and Parmesan.

To finish, add the pickles and butter to the shrimp. Season with salt, pepper, and lemon juice to taste. Serve over the grits and garnish with tarragon.

For the grits:

3 cups (720 ml) cold milk

1 cup (240 ml) cold water

1 teaspoon salt

1 cup (112 g) instant grits

4 tablespoons (2 ounces/ 55 g) unsalted butter

½ cup (50 g) finely grated Parmesan cheese

For finishing:

¼ cup (70 g) chopped Grillo's spicy pickles

½ stick (1 ounce/28 g) butter

Salt and freshly ground black pepper

1 tablespoon fresh lemon juice, or to taste

¼ cup (11 g) chopped fresh tarragon

UKRAINIAN SOLYANKA

Serves 4

One of Chef Raph's family recipes, this hearty soup certainly encourages slurping. Cozy up with a cup or a big fat bowl and dig in.

Ingredients

- 2 tablespoons vegetable oil
- 1 pound (16 ounces/455 g) kielbasa, sliced into coins
- 2 pounds (32 ounces/910 g) beef chuck steak, cut into 1-inch (2.5 cm) pieces
- ½ pound (8 ounces/225 g) smoked ham, cut into ½-inch (12 mm) pieces
- 1 cup (60 g) sliced cremini mushrooms
- ¼ cup (35 g) pitted olives, halved
- 2 cups (220 g) roughly diced onions
- 1 cup (140 g) diced carrots
- 2 tablespoons tomato paste
- Salt and freshly ground black pepper
- 1 tablespoon ground allspice
- 2 bay leaves
- 4 cups (950 ml) chicken stock
- 2 cups (480 ml) Grillo's pickle brine
- 1 cup (280 g) roughly chopped Grillo's pickles
- ½ cup (120 ml) sour cream
- ¼ cup (13 g) chopped fresh dill
- ¼ cup (9 g) chopped fresh parsley
- 1 lemon, quartered

In a large soup pot, heat the oil over medium heat. Add the kielbasa, beef, and ham and cook until golden brown, about 10 minutes. Add the mushrooms, olives, onions, and carrots and continue to sauté for another 10 minutes. Stir in the tomato paste, 1 tablespoon salt, 1 teaspoon pepper, the allspice, and bay leaves. Reduce the heat to low and cook until aromatic, about 5 minutes.

Add the chicken stock, 2 cups (480 ml) water, and the pickle brine and scrape the bottom of the pan to get up any browned bits and deglaze the pan. Reduce the heat to low, cover, and simmer for 1½ hours.

To serve, spoon into soup bowls and garnish with the chopped pickles, sour cream, dill, and parsley and the lemon quarters alongside for squeezing.

SAM SAM'S

FUN FACT #1

SO MANY GREATS HAVE COME OUT OF BROOKLYN AND THE PICKLEBACK SHOT IS NO EXCEPTION! A SHOT OF WHISKEY WITH A PICKLE BRINE CHASER AND THE WORLD HAS NEVER BEEN THE SAME. LEGEND HAS IT THAT THE PICKLEBACK WAS INVENTED BY A BROOKLYN BARTENDER NAMED REGGIE CUNNINGHAM IN 2006 WHEN AT THE BUSHWICK COUNTRY CLUB WHERE HE WAS WORKING, HE WAS APPROACHED BY A WOMAN—WITH A GOLD TOOTH—WHO INSISTED THAT HE DO A SERIES OF WHISKEY SHOTS WITH HER, FOLLOWED BY PICKLE BRINE. HE AGREED, AND, AS HE PUT IT: "THE REST IS HISTORY."

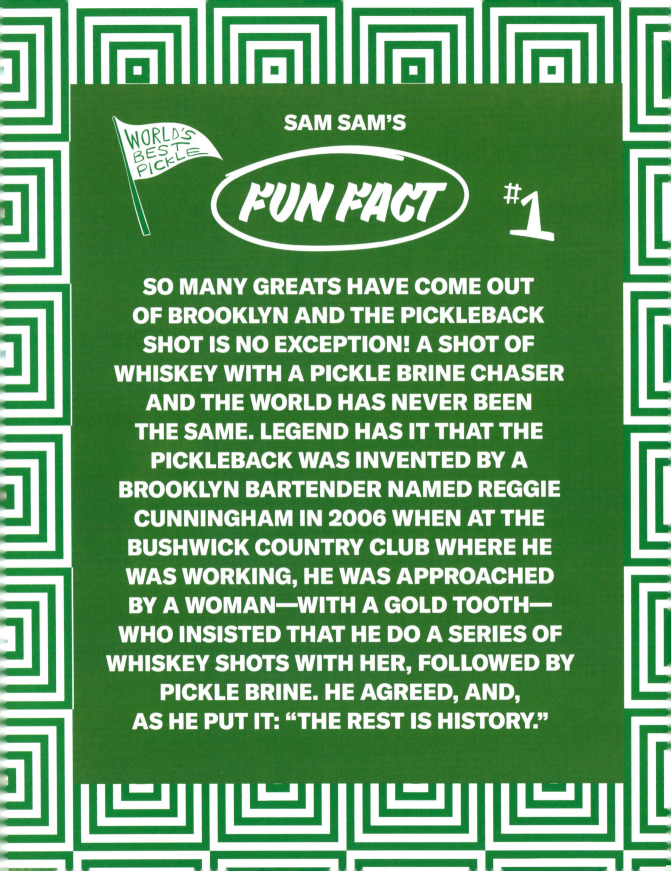

Chapter 8

HAPPY HOUR

When you're talking pickles it's happy hour 24/7/365. Luckily, due to how dope pickles are, making a great drink is actually pretty easy when you incorporate some fresh brine or pickles into the mix. The real bonus is that pickle juice is the gift the keeps on giving—whether it be cocktails at night or a hangover cure in the morning. How can you hate on something with a built-in support system like that? We're willing to bet that they'd even slip that cute girl your number or hold your hair back if they could!

PICKLE SIMPLE SYRUP

Makes 1⅓ cups (315 ml)

Why would you bother with plain simple syrup when you can make it this special? You can add your pickle simple syrup to cocktails, desserts, and everything in between!

Ingredients

- 1 cup (200 g) granulated sugar
- ½ cup (120 ml) Grillo's pickle brine or Basic Brine (page 20)

In a saucepan, combine the sugar, brine, and ½ cup (120 ml) water and bring to a boil. Whisk until the sugar fully dissolves. Allow the syrup to fully cool before using.

HANGOVER CURE

Serves 4

Did you know pickle juice actually contains more electrolytes than Gatorade? You'll thank us later.

In an ice-filled cocktail shaker, combine the egg yolk, liquor, pickle brine, and lemon juice. Shake vigorously for 1 minute, until chilled and well emulsified. Divide evenly among 4 rocks glasses with one-half of an Alka-Seltzer tablet in each. Garnish each glass with an oyster and a dash of Tabasco.

Ingredients

1 large egg yolk

¼ cup (60 ml) Pickle-Infused Liquor (page 174)

1 tablespoon Grillo's pickle brine

1 tablespoon fresh lemon juice

2 Alka Seltzer tablets, broken in half

4 oysters, shucked

Tabasco hot sauce

THE PERFECT BLOODY MARY

Makes 4 cocktails

If you say "pickle juice" five times in the mirror this drink may appear.

In a pitcher, combine the tomato juice, vodka, pickle brine, celery seeds, Worcestershire sauce, horseradish, and celery salt. Add ice and shake for a minute until chilled and well incorporated. Wet the rim of a highball glass with a pickle chip and rim the glass with Tajín. Pour the drink mixture into a highball glass. Garnish with your favorite toppings (we love bacon and a fried pickle chip).

Ingredients

4 cups (950 ml) tomato juice

1 cup (240 ml) vodka

⅓ cup (75 ml) Grillo's pickle brine or Basic Brine (page 20)

1 teaspoon celery seeds

1 teaspoon Worcestershire sauce

1 teaspoon prepared horseradish

¼ teaspoon celery salt

4 Grillo's pickle chips

1 tablespoon Tajín seasoning

Your favorite garnishes

PICKLE-INFUSED LIQUOR

Makes 2 cups (480 ml)

Sometimes you get a little pickled. Why not do it with pickle-infused cocktails? This recipe takes just two easy steps and can be a great addition to your home bar.

Pour the vodka over the pickles in an airtight container. Store in the refrigerator for 5 days and you will be left with pickle-infused liquor.

Ingredients

2 cups (480 ml) vodka (or any clear liquor)

1 cup (210 g) Grillo's pickle chips

GRILLO'S PICKLES
FRESH
Pickle Spears
CLASSIC DILL
32 FL OZ (1 QT) 946 mL
Nutrition Facts

PICKLEBACK SLUSH

Makes 4 cocktails

These pickles came to party. A new take on the pickleback shot, these slushies are perfect for kicking back and chilling out.

Pour the pickle brine into a standard ice cube tray (2 tablespoons per cube) and freeze.

In a high-powered blender, combine the brine cubes, whiskey, lime juice, simple syrup, and ginger ale and blend until a slushy consistency.

Ingredients

1½ cups (360 ml) Grillo's pickle brine or Basic Brine (page 20)

½ cup (120 ml) whiskey

¼ cup (60 ml) fresh lime juice

2 tablespoons Pickle Simple Syrup (page 170)

¼ cup (60 ml) ginger ale

SAM SAM'S FAVORITE SODA

Makes 4 drinks

Pickle soda? Pickle pop? Whatever you want to call it, we love it.

Pour the seltzer water into ice-filled glasses. Finish with some simple syrup and garnish with a pickle spear.

Ingredients

3½ cups (849 ml) seltzer water

Ice

½ cup (120 ml) Pickle Simple Syrup (page 170)

4 Grillo's pickle spears

GRILLO'S
PICKLES

TRO-PICKLE MARGARITAS

Makes 4 cocktails

We can all agree that margaritas rule. Sweet, savory, or sour, they're the perfect drink to have when you want to chill out and relax. Pickle juice + tequila = yes, please.

Fill a pitcher with the crushed ice, tequila, lime juice, pickle brine, and simple syrup and mix until cold. Rim the glasses with lime wedges and roll in the Tajín. Garnish each glass with a lime.

Ingredients

- 2 cups (480 ml) crushed ice
- 1 cup (240 ml) tequila blanco
- ½ cup (120 ml) fresh lime juice
- ¼ cup (60 ml) Grillo's pickle brine or Basic Brine (page 20)
- ¼ cup (60 ml) Pickle Simple Syrup (page 170)
- Lime wedges, for rimming the glasses and for garnish
- 1 cup (48 g) Tajín seasoning, for rimming the glasses

GRILLO'S SIGNATURE MARTINIS

Makes 4 cocktails

If you want a dirty, absolutely filthy, martini, pickle juice is the way to go. This martini will have you questioning why you ever put an olive in there in the first place.

Thread 3 pickle chips onto each of the skewers and set aside. Set 4 martini glasses in the freezer to chill.

In an ice-filled cocktail shaker, combine the vodka, vermouth, and pickle brine. Shake vigorously for 1 minute, until the drink is chilled and well blended. Strain into the chilled glasses and garnish with the pickle chip skewers.

Ingredients

- 4 small wooden skewers
- 12 Grillo's pickle chips, for garnish
- ½ cup (120 ml) vodka
- ½ cup (120 ml) dry vermouth
- 2 tablespoons Grillo's pickle brine

GRILLO'S PICKLES

SAM SAM'S

FUN FACT

DO YOU KNOW WHAT THE BEST DAY OF THE YEAR IS? IT'S NATIONAL PICKLE DAY ON NOVEMBER 14. THIS IS THE PERFECT COOKBOOK FOR THROWING A PICKLE PARTY.

Chapter 9

SWEET (AND SOUR) TREATS

Pickles and desserts are not something typically used in the same sentence . . . never mind in the same recipe. These treats will have you questioning reality because combining pickles and sweet desserts is about to become your new love language. Our Utah Pickle Pie (page 195) is as wacky as it sounds, and our Pickle Pops (page 187) will have you yearning for the sticky heat of summer all year round. These are THE ultimate sweet offerings for your taste buds, and as Marie Antoinette (never actually) said, "Let them eat Pickle Pineapple Upside Down Cake!"

PICKLE POPS

Makes 8 pops

Popsicles have always been a top-tier summer treat. Pickles and pops?! That sounds like a childhood dream come true.

PRO TIP: *Have one after a workout to help restore electrolytes and cool you down.*

In a container with a pour spout, combine the pickle brine, simply syrup, whiskey, and lime juice. Pour into 8 ice pop molds. Freeze overnight and enjoy.

Ingredients

2 cups (480 ml) Grillo's pickle brine or Basic Brine (page 20)

½ cup (120 ml) Pickle Simple Syrup (page 170)

½ cup (120 ml) Jameson Irish whiskey

1 tablespoon fresh lime juice

PICKLE ICE CREAM

Serves 4

I scream, you scream, we all scream for pickle ice cream! Now sit down and consider your cravings satisfied.

In a medium saucepan, combine the cream, milk, sugar, and egg yolks and whisk over medium heat until the custard has thickened, about 10 minutes. Refrigerate until fully cooled.

Whisk in the pickle brine and food coloring. Churn in an ice cream maker according to the manufacturer's instructions until it is nice and creamy. Eat right away!

Ingredients

2 cups (480 ml) heavy cream

¾ cup (180 ml) whole milk

¾ cup (150 g) sugar

4 large egg yolks

¾ cup (180 ml) Grillo's pickle brine or Basic Brine (page 20)

4 dashes of green food coloring

PICKLE PINEAPPLE UPSIDE DOWN CAKE

Serves 4

We really turned this classic dessert upside down by adding a briny kick. Quick, say "pickle pineapple" three times fast:
Pickle Pineapple
Pickle Pineapple
Pickle Pineapple

Ingredients

- ½ stick (2 ounces/55 g) butter, melted
- 1 cup (220 g) packed brown sugar
- 10 canned pineapple rings
- 10 Grillo's pickle chips
- 1 box yellow cake mix
- ½ cup (120 ml) vegetable oil
- 3 large eggs
- ½ cup (120 ml) Grillo's pickle brine or Basic Brine (page 20)

Preheat the oven to 350°F (180°C).

Pour the melted butter into a 13 by 9-inch (33 by 23 cm) baking pan. Sprinkle the brown sugar evenly over the buttered pan. Arrange the pineapple rings over the sugar. Place a pickle chip in the center of each pineapple ring.

In a bowl, whisk together the cake mix, vegetable oil, eggs, ½ cup (120 ml) water, and the pickle brine until well incorporated. Pour the batter over the pineapples in the baking pan.

Transfer to the oven and bake until set, about 45 minutes. Allow to cool for 30 minutes, then flip the cake out of the pan onto a serving platter.

Pickle Pineapple Upside Down Cake (page 189)

FUNNEL CAKES

Serves 4

These funnel cakes won first prize at the carnival. With its delectable salty and sweet flavor, we barely even had to bribe the judges!

Pour 6 inches (15 cm) oil into a dutch oven and heat to 375°F (190°C).

In a medium bowl, whisk together the flour, sugar, baking powder, and salt until fully combined. In a separate bowl, whisk together the milk and eggs. Gradually pour the milk mixture into the flour mixture and whisk until well combined.

Drizzle the batter into the oil, crisscrossing the batter onto itself. Fry for 90 seconds per side.

Serve topped with the simple syrup and a sprinkling of powdered sugar.

Ingredients

Vegetable oil, for deep-frying

2 cups (250 g) all-purpose flour

2 tablespoons granulated sugar

1 teaspoon baking powder

1 teaspoon salt

1 cup (240 ml) whole milk

2 large eggs

2 tablespoons Pickle Simple Syrup (page 170)

2 tablespoons powdered sugar

GRILLO'S
PICKLES

UTAH PICKLE PIE

Serves 6

From the tiny town of Bicknell, Utah, to your table, this pickle pie will turn heads and change your perspective on pickles forever!

Ingredients

- 3 tablespoons potato starch
- 1½ cups (300 g) sugar
- 5 large eggs
- 1 cup (240 ml) half-and-half
- ½ stick (2 ounces/55 g) unsalted melted butter
- 2 teaspoons grated lemon zest
- ¼ teaspoon ground nutmeg
- 1 cup (280 g) chopped Grillo's pickles
- 1 (9-inch/23 cm) frozen pie crust, thawed
- 1½ cups (360 ml) whipped cream
- 6 Grillo's pickle chips

Preheat the oven to 350°F (180°C).

In a stand mixer fitted with the whisk, whip together 2 tablespoons of the potato starch, the sugar, eggs, and half-and-half until creamy. Add the melted butter, lemon zest, and nutmeg and mix until well combined. Fold in the chopped pickles and the remaining 1 tablespoon potato starch and pour into the pie shell.

Bake until set, about 1 hour. Let it cool on a wire rack and refrigerate for at least 2 hours.

To serve, top the pie with whipped cream and pickle chips.

Super Fresh Super Crispy

World's Best Pickle

SAM SAM'S

FUN FACT

IT IS SAID THAT YOU CAN HEAR THE CRUNCH OF A GOOD PICKLE FROM TEN PACES. THE CRUNCH OF A GREAT PICKLE CAN BE HEARD FROM TWENTY PACES AND GRILLO'S PASSED THE TEST!

CHILL OUT
→ HAVE A PICKLE

Chapter 10

SAUCES AND SPREADS

Just like pickles, condiments can tie an entire recipe together, but are often overlooked. Ketchup and french fries, chips and salsa, pickles and, well, everything. These iconic pairings have brought smiles to people's faces for centuries. Sorry for your new obsession. These sauces and spreads will have a permanent space in your fridge, so make sure to clear a shelf—come on, we both know you aren't going to drink that ginger shot that's been sitting there since New Year's.

Pimento 5/4
P. Mayo 5/4
P. mustard 5/4
Chimi 5/4
tar tar 5/4
BBQ 5/4

Green goddess 5/4
Ranch 5/4
Tahini Gochu Garu 5/4
Relish 5/4
P. Vin 5/4
Dill pickle Dip 5/3

PIMENTO CHEESE SPREAD

Makes 3 cups (720 ml)

- 2 cups (230 g) shredded extra-sharp Cheddar cheese
- 8 ounces (225 g) cream cheese, at room temperature
- ½ cup (120 ml) mayonnaise
- ½ cup (120 g) chopped roasted peppers
- ½ cup (140 g) chopped Grillo's pickles
- ½ teaspoon garlic powder
- ½ teaspoon onion powder
- ½ teaspoon cayenne pepper
- ½ teaspoon paprika
- Salt and freshly ground black pepper

In a bowl, combine the Cheddar, cream cheese, mayonnaise, roasted peppers, pickles, garlic powder, onion powder, cayenne pepper, paprika, and salt and black pepper to taste and mix well until creamy. Refrigerate for up to 1 week.

BEST PICKLE MAYO

Makes 2 cups (480 ml)

- 2 large egg yolks
- 2 cups (240 ml) vegetable oil
- ½ teaspoon Dijon mustard
- 1 teaspoon fresh lemon juice
- 1 teaspoon champagne vinegar
- 1 tablespoon pickle juice
- ½ teaspoon salt

In a tall container (or the cup for an immersion blender), combine the egg yolks, oil, mustard, lemon juice, vinegar, pickle juice, and salt and emulsify with an immersion blender. Store in an airtight container in the refrigerator for up to 1 week.

GREEN GODDESS DRESSING

Makes 2 cups (480 ml)

1 cup (240 ml) buttermilk

½ cup (110 g) mayonnaise

⅓ cup (50 g) cubed avocado

2 tablespoons Grillo's pickle brine

1 tablespoon fresh lemon juice

¼ cup (70 g) chopped Grillo's pickles

1 tablespoon fresh chopped jalapeño

1 peeled whole garlic clove

½ cup (17 g) chopped fresh parsley

½ cup (23 g) chopped fresh chives

½ cup (25 g) chopped fresh dill

½ cup (25 g) chopped fresh tarragon

1 tablespoon freshly ground black pepper

Salt

In a blender, combine the buttermilk, mayonnaise, avocado, pickle brine, lemon juice, chopped pickles, jalapeño, garlic, the fresh herbs, and black pepper. Blend on high until completely smooth. Season with salt to taste. Adjust the consistency with water if needed. Store in an airtight container in the refrigerator for up to 3 days.

GRILLO'S RANCH

Makes 2 cups (480 ml)

1 cup (240 ml) sour cream

½ cup (110 g) mayonnaise

½ cup (120 ml) buttermilk

2 tablespoons Grillo's pickle brine or Basic Brine (page 20)

1 tablespoon fresh lemon juice

1 teaspoon freshly ground black pepper

1 teaspoon onion powder

1 teaspoon garlic powder

1 garlic clove, grated on a Microplane

Salt

In a medium bowl, stir together the sour cream, mayonnaise, buttermilk, pickle brine, lemon juice, pepper, onion powder, garlic powder, garlic, and salt to taste. Whisk until fully incorporated. Store in an airtight container in the refrigerator for up to 2 weeks.

PICKLE MUSTARD

Makes 2 cups (480 ml)

- 1½ cups (360 ml) yellow mustard
- 3 tablespoons Dijon mustard
- 1 tablespoon honey
- ¼ cup (70 g) chopped Grillo's pickles
- 1 teaspoon sherry vinegar

In a bowl, whisk both mustards, the honey, pickles, and vinegar until combined. Refrigerate for up to 1 week.

PICKLE CHIMICHURRI

Makes 2 cups (480 ml)

- 1 cup (240 ml) olive oil
- 2 tablespoons Grillo's pickle brine
- 2 tablespoons red wine vinegar
- ½ cup (17 g) finely chopped fresh parsley
- ¼ cup (70 g) chopped Grillo's pickles
- ¼ cup (11 g) chopped fresh chives
- 3 garlic cloves, minced
- 1 tablespoon minced seeded Fresno chile
- 1 teaspoon dried oregano
- 1 teaspoon crushed red pepper flakes
- 1 teaspoon freshly ground black pepper

In a bowl, stir together the oil, pickle brine, vinegar, parsley, chopped pickles, chives, garlic, chile, oregano, pepper flakes, and black pepper until well combined. Store in an airtight container in the refrigerator for up to 1 week.

GREEN RELISH

Makes 2 cups (480 ml)

- 1½ cups (420 g) chopped Grillo's pickles
- ½ cup (65 g) finely chopped onion
- 2 teaspoons Pickled Mustard Seeds (page 26)
- 2 tablespoons Grillo's pickle brine
- 2 tablespoons apple cider vinegar
- 4 dashes of green food coloring
- 2 tablespoons sugar
- 1 teaspoon celery seeds
- 1 teaspoon salt

In a medium bowl, combine the chopped pickles, onion, mustard seeds, pickle brine, vinegar, food coloring, sugar, celery seeds, and salt until well combined. Store in an airtight container in the refrigerator for up to 2 months.

PICKLE TIME TARTAR SAUCE

Makes 2 cups (480 ml)

- 1¼ cups (300 ml) mayonnaise
- ½ cup (120 ml) crème fraîche
- ¼ cup (70 g) chopped Grillo's pickles
- 1 tablespoon minced fresh chives
- 1½ teaspoons fresh lemon juice
- ½ teaspoon Worcestershire sauce
- ½ teaspoon cayenne pepper

In a small bowl, combine the mayonnaise, crème fraîche, pickles, chives, lemon juice, Worcestershire sauce, and cayenne until well incorporated. It should have a nice and creamy texture. Store in an airtight container in the refrigerator for up to 2 weeks.

PICKLE BBQ SAUCE

Makes 2 cups (480 ml)

- 1 tablespoon vegetable oil
- ½ cup (65 g) chopped onion
- ¼ cup (35 g) minced garlic
- 1 cup (240 ml) ketchup
- ½ cup (110 g) packed brown sugar
- 1 cup (240 ml) apple cider vinegar
- ½ cup (120 ml) lager
- ¼ cup (60 ml) Grillo's pickle brine
- ¼ cup (70 g) chopped Grillo's pickles
- 3 tablespoons Worcestershire sauce
- 2 tablespoons garlic powder
- 2 tablespoons onion powder
- 1 teaspoon ground coriander
- 1 teaspoon ground cumin
- 1 tablespoon paprika
- 1 teaspoon freshly ground black pepper

In a medium saucepan, heat the oil over medium-low heat. Add the onion and garlic and sauté until translucent, about 10 minutes.

Add the ketchup, brown sugar, vinegar, lager, pickle brine, pickles, Worcestershire sauce, garlic powder, onion powder, coriander, cumin, paprika, and black pepper. Cook over low heat for 30 minutes, stirring frequently.

Let cool and store in an airtight container in the refrigerator for up to 2 days.

EVERYDAY PICKLE VINAIGRETTE

Makes 2 cups (480 ml)

- 1½ cups (360 ml) Grillo's pickle brine or Basic Brine (page 20)
- ½ cup (120 ml) vegetable oil
- ½ cup (120 ml) champagne vinegar
- 2 teaspoons Dijon mustard
- 1 peeled whole garlic clove
- ¼ cup (13 g) chopped fresh dill
- Salt

In a blender, combine the pickle brine, oil, vinegar, mustard, garlic, and dill and blend on high until emulsified. Season with salt to taste. Store in an airtight container in the refrigerator for up to 1 week.

DILL PICKLE DIP

Makes 2½ cups (600 ml)

8 ounces (225 g) cream cheese, at room temperature

½ cup (120 ml) sour cream

¾ cup (210 g) chopped Grillo's pickles

2 tablespoons Grillo's pickle brine

1 tablespoon chopped fresh dill

1 teaspoon garlic powder

Salt

In a bowl, combine the cream cheese, sour cream, pickles, pickle brine, dill, garlic powder, and salt to taste and mix with a wooden spoon. Store in an airtight container in the refrigerator for up to 3 days.

TAHINI GOCHUGARU DIP

Makes 1 cup (240 ml)

½ cup (140 g) chopped Grillo's dill pickles, drained

½ cup (120 ml) tahini

2 tablespoons fresh lime juice

1 tablespoon gochujang

1 tablespoon gochugaru

1 tablespoon rice vinegar

1 tablespoon togarashi

¼ cup (60 ml) warm water, or as needed

In a large bowl, whisk together the pickles, tahini, lime juice, gochujang, gochugaru, vinegar, and togarashi. Add the warm water as needed to ensure a smooth texture. Store in an airtight container in the refrigerator for up to 1 week.

PICKLE HERB BUTTER

Makes 2 cups (445 g)

- 3 sticks (12 ounces/340 g) unsalted butter, at room temperature
- ¼ cup (70 g) chopped Grillo's pickles, drained
- 1 tablespoon finely chopped fresh chives
- 1 tablespoon finely chopped fresh dill
- 1 tablespoon finely chopped fresh thyme
- 1 garlic clove, minced
- 1 teaspoon salt

In a bowl, stir together the butter, pickles, chives, dill, thyme, garlic, and salt until well incorporated. Lay a sheet of plastic wrap on a flat surface place the butter mixture in the center. Roll the plastic wrap over the butter and press it into a log shape. Twirl the ends of the plastic wrap and tuck them under the roll. Place it in the fridge for at least 2 hours or overnight until the butter is solid again.

Slice and serve! Refrigerate for up to 2 weeks.

GRILLO'S BURGER SAUCE

Makes 2 cups (480 ml)

- ⅔ cup (165 ml) mayonnaise
- ⅔ cup (165 ml) ketchup
- ¼ cup (60 ml) yellow mustard
- 1 tablespoon Grillo's spicy pickle brine
- 1 tablespoon hot sauce
- ½ teaspoon garlic powder
- ½ teaspoon onion powder
- ½ teaspoon paprika
- ½ teaspoon sugar
- ¼ cup (70 g) chopped Grillo's spicy pickles

In a medium bowl, whisk together the mayonnaise, ketchup, mustard, pickle brine, hot sauce, garlic powder, onion powder, paprika, and sugar. Fold in the chopped pickles. Store in an airtight container for up to 3 days.

FLAMING PICKLE HOT SAUCE

Makes 2 cups (480 ml)

- 1½ cups (360 ml) Grillo's pickle brine
- 2 tablespoons honey
- ½ cup (140 grams) chopped Grillo's pickles
- 2 jalapeños, deseeded and chopped
- 1 teaspoon coriander
- 1 teaspoon cumin
- 1 tablespoon red pepper flakes
- Salt

In a blender, add the pickle brine, honey, chopped pickles, jalapeños, coriander, cumin, and red pepper flakes and blend on high until fully emulsified. Add salt to taste. Strain through a fine-mesh sieve and store in an airtight container in the refrigerator for up to 2 months.

PICKLE NACHO CHEESE

Makes 3 cups (720 ml)

- 1 cup (240 ml) whole milk
- ¼ cup (60 ml) Grillo's pickle brine
- 1 cup (110 g) Velveeta, cubed
- 1 cup (110 g) shredded pepper jack cheese
- ¼ cup (70 g) chopped Grillo's Pickle de Gallo
- 1 teaspoon garlic powder
- 2 teaspoons chipotle powder
- 1 teaspoon Tajín seasoning
- Salt

In a medium saucepan, bring the milk and pickle brine to a boil. Reduce to a simmer and slowly whisk in the Velveeta and pepper jack cheese. Once a sauce consistency has formed add the Pickle de Gallo, garlic powder, chipotle powder, Tajín, and salt to taste.

GRILLO'S
NY SMOKING GUN
GRILLO'S PICKLES
末広がり
TWO JAMES SP
JOHN
SMOK
87 PROO

SPECIAL ACKNOWLEDGMENTS

This book wouldn't be possible without the love and support of our friends, family, and everyone who has invited Grillo's Pickles into their hearts, homes, and refrigerators.

Thank you to Short Stories, Chef Raphael Khutorsky, Chef Sam Medrano, Ilan Khutorsky, and Jeckson Leonardo for your time and dedication to this book.

SPECIAL THANKS

Ceara Perez-Murphy: coeditor, copywriter, friend, lifesaver
Rob Soucy: copywriter and friend
Eddie Mellow: copywriter

GRILLO'S
PICKLES
I
GRILLO'S
PICKLES

HIGH
GRILLO'S PICKLES
NEWKS
HOT SAUCE
REFRIGERATE AFTER OPENING
KITCHEN

GRILLO'S PICKLES
Pickle Spears
CH
EAT
FIND US CH
0094
LISION
AR RENTAL
K
KENSCOLLISION

LL OUT &
A PICKLE
N IN THE REFRIGERATED SECTION
TFRONT
AGUA DE SAN PEDRO
954

I ♥ GRILLO'S PICKLES

PHOTO AND ART CREDITS

JUSTIN AHARONI

pages 4, 12, 18–19, 21, 24, 30, 32, 34, 36–37, 42–43, 44, 46, 48, 58, 61, 66, 69, 70, 74–75, 77, 80, 82, 87, 89, 90, 93, 95, 96, 102, 104, 106, 108–109, 111, 112, 115, 116, 120–121, 122, 125, 130, 132–133, 136, 142–143, 145, 146, 151, 153, 154, 157, 159, 160–161, 162, 164, 175, 176, 179, 180, 186, 190–191, 192, 194, 198–199, 222

EDDIE ANDRE

pages 15, 222–223

LUIS ANTONIO

pages 22, 50, 54, 56–57, 62, 78, 98, 129, 138, 173, 183

MATTHEW LANGILLE

page 52 (left)

MATTHEW ROULAN

pages 210–211

IAN SHIVER

pages 8, 216

NICK ZAREMBA

pages 5, 10, 16, 28, 52 (right), 84, 100, 126, 148, 169, 170, 171, 178, 184, 196

TO CLOSE: PRESS DOWN FIRMLY ON THE EDGES OF CONTAINER
GRILLO'S PICKLES
FRESH
Italian Dill Spears

INDEX

H

I

J

K

L

M

N

O

GRILLO'S
PICKLES

GRILLO'S PICKLES
GRILLO'S PICKLES
R
D
GRILLO'S PICKLES

Editors: Juliet Dore and Asha Simon
Designer: Heesang Lee
Managing Editor: Annalea Manalili
Production Managers: Larry Pekarek and Kathleen Gaffney

Library of Congress Control Number: 2023950281

ISBN: 978-1-4197-7188-0
eISBN: 979-8-88707-211-1

For photo and art credits, see page 215

Printed and bound in China
10 9 8 7 6 5 4 3 2 1

ABRAMS The Art of Books
195 Broadway, New York, NY 10007
abramsbooks.com

GRILLO'S PICKLES
I ♥ GRILLO'S PICKLES
GRILLO'S

I ♥ GRILLO'S PICKLES
GRILLO'S PICKLES